**D0260584**

**Jonat**

Oxfo

Univ

engir

a mar

in Eu

medi

Lond

refer

publi

Direc

Oxfo

In hi

coach

shops

uates

progr

He w

Servi

confe

resea

gradu

# Where am I Going and Can I Have a Map?

*Jonathan Black*

..............

**A How To Book**

Leabharlanna Poiblí Chathair Baile Átha Cliath
Dublin City Public Libraries

ROBINSON

First published in Great Britain in 2017 by
Robinson

A CIP catalogue record for this book
is available from the British Library.

ISBN 978-1-47213-758-6

Typeset by Hewer Text UK Ltd, Edinburgh
Printed and bound in Great Britain by CPI
Group (UK) Ltd, Croydon CR0 4YY

Papers used by Robinson are from well-
managed forests and other responsible
sources

MIX
Paper from
responsible sources
FSC
www.fsc.org FSC® C104740

Robinson
An imprint of
Little, Brown Book Group
Carmelite House
50 Victoria Embankment
London EC4Y 0DZ

An Hachette UK Company
www.hachette.co.uk

www.littlebrown.co.uk

How To Books are published by
Robinson, an imprint of Little, Brown
Book Group. We welcome proposals
from authors who have first-hand
experience of their subjects. Please set
out the aims of your book, its target
market and its suggested contents in an
email to Nikki.Read@howtobooks.co.uk

To Nicky, Alex and Immy – for their
inspiration and encouragement

# Contents

# Preface

In this book, I show you how you can step back from your current job worries and think about your career within the arc of your life. I include some statistics and sociological research where it is helpful, and sprinkle in many real examples to bring it all alive.

It's not all theory; I describe some invaluable tools that you could use right now if you want to, or store away until you, or a friend or relative, could use them. I'm sorry to say that there are no easy answers (well, none worth having), no computer programs or apps to do the work for you – but I think that's the real fun of life, and with this book in your career toolbox, you'll be ready. After all, since it could help you work out how to spend at least the next three years, it's probably worth spending some time on thinking about your career, especially when you'd spend many hours on an essay, project or dissertation that are forgotten after three weeks.

I wrote this book primarily for those of you who are students about to leave the fixed routines of school, university or college; however, I think it will also provide valuable encouragement for those of you changing jobs or thinking you are underemployed and really wouldn't mind a change. Finally, I believe the information given here can be useful for everyone wanting to help, especially friends and family. While some aspects of job-hunting have not changed, many aspects of finding a job or thinking about a career really are 'not like it was in my day'.

I meet many students who confide in the Careers Service team about wanting to try a job of which they think their parents won't immediately approve; I hope that this book might provide some friendly common ground between anxious job seekers and their enthusiastic supporters.

# Foreword

Whether you find the career question just overwhelming, or you genuinely want to answer it but can't think how to, I'd suggest there are ways you can think about it in smaller steps.

How can you decide on a career? Consider these three approaches and see which you'd prefer: first, the Lucky Dip. Open a career directory at random and select the first job you come to – any good? Car manufacturer? Coal miner? Tax accountant? Deep-sea fisherman? Arbitrage trader? While these are great jobs for someone, they are probably not exactly what you are after. You'll see that the 'All my friends are applying for . . .' more or less falls into this category.

Second approach: the Blinding Light. Here the idea is that you wait for inspiration to strike you – the thing is that success with this approach is really rare, perhaps the last recorded event like this was 2000 years ago on the road to Damascus, or before that with Archimedes' Eureka moment.

So we have a third approach and, as you might guess, the one to use when the Lucky Dip and Blinding Light approaches have not delivered and you don't want to wait any longer: a Map.

And, since this might take some time, you'll appreciate some resilience, creativity and persistence – good skills for a job, as it happens. In fact, sometimes looking for a job is a job itself.

The book is divided into three parts. You can read it from beginning to end (it does make sense that way), but you can also dive into specific sections if, for example, you immediately want some advice on your CV, or you want to work out where you want to be in five years' time.

In Part One, I'll discuss the bigger issues that frame the whole area of careers and jobs.

In Part Two of this book, I'll start to move on to the practicalities.

Finally in Part Three, I'll discuss how to cope with the hurdles and challenges that you might encounter while you're travelling along the map.

# An aerial view – what's this all about?

....................

## THE VIEW OF THE MAP FROM 10,000 FEET

When you're down on the ground, following the detailed map, along pathways and round obstacles, you may not have a clear view of where you want to be in a day, a year, or even in five years' time. You may wonder why this map, this direction or this target? You can't see the targets or all the pathways to get there.

Part One is the helicopter that will raise you up above the map to give you that aerial view so you can answer the big questions and set your overall direction – where, roughly, am I going? What is my aim? How long have I got? How do I start? I've got no choice, or I've got too many choices. Do I follow what other people have told me to do and where I should go?

This first section won't help with the day-to-day practicalities of finding and getting a job – that's for Part Two – but it's arguably more important as a way to help you lay out your overall map, set the boundaries, and your personal targets. You don't need to read this section first, but you may well come back to it as you start to follow the first pathways of your career map.

Let's start: forget the details of how to write a CV for now, and hover up to view the whole map that covers the next one, five, or ten years.

## NO 'RIGHT' ANSWERS

If you think about it, all through school you are marked on what you do. Even outside the classroom there are scores or marks, whether it's sport or music, drama or ballet. It's clear to everyone what 'good' looks like – a high score is a good thing. You may, however, be involved in activities that aren't scored – volunteering at the local community centre, helping others to gain a skill (like reading or maths), washing the dishes.

When you leave school, perhaps going into an apprenticeship, into work or into university, you probably started doing more things that weren't scored, where it wasn't clear or agreed what was 'right' or 'good'. In fact, you probably got involved in activities just because you enjoyed them – perhaps like your early childhood.

Careers and jobs are challenging because there are *no right answers*, though some people think there must be – or they set targets for themselves so that they can then judge their jobs and give themselves a score.

A few months ago, a student came to me asking if the job he had in mind would be 'right'.

I asked him, 'What do you mean? What does "right" look like, how would you measure it?'

He thought for a moment and answered, 'It's with an organisation that my friends have heard of, well paid, interesting work, and in London.'

'Well, that's a clear answer and gives you four measures by which you'll be able to check each job you apply for,' I said. 'But, of course, it begs more questions: what does "well paid" mean? What makes work "interesting"? Just because your friends have heard of the organisation, does that mean anything?'

Your proposed job is not something you can score – this job gets 73 per cent or an A* – I know it's unusual but there is no 'right' answer to what is a good job or career. Only you can tell what's right for you; however, I can tell you what some students at Oxford reported was important to them in a job and you can see if you agree.

We surveyed 850 undergraduate students from all years and all subjects; we asked them to score on a scale from 1 (not important) to 6 (very important) how important were each of ten aspects of a job. The average score for each aspect is shown in the graph below.

What can we tell from this? Intellectual challenge is top – the aspect that will, to coin a phrase, 'get you out of bed in the morning' and certainly sustain you. I'm unclear what 'Work/life

The intellectual challenge of the role — 4.84

Work/life balance — 4.58

Location — 4.35

Security of employment — 4.30

That it's a cause I feel good about or that I am serving the greater good — 4.25

High level of pay — 4.01

Availability of funding (especially for postgraduate study) — 3.73

Starting a role where I believe I'd be able to have a family and a career, even if not right now — 3.46

The chance to join a formal graduate training programme — 3.43

My partner's plans — 2.58

balance' means; when I've talked to sixth-formers about this they say, 'If I'm working on a supermarket checkout, then that's Work and I'd want a Life separately. But if I'm in an interesting job, then it wouldn't be so important to have such a separate "Life" part.'

That seems to make sense: for an interesting job, work and life merge – perhaps not always for the best. With today's mobile phones and perpetual connection to the office through email and mobile phones, then your challenge is how to switch off from work and get refreshed.

Note the fifth item on the list: 'A cause I feel good about, or serving the greater good'. If you split the chart and data between men and women, this is the item that women feel much more strongly about than men (men feel stronger about 'High level of pay' . . .).

At and near the bottom of the list, with the lowest priorities, are 'Starting a role where I believe I'd be able to have a family and a career, even if not right now' and 'My partner's plans'. While some organisations and industries are more 'family friendly' than others, there is basic legislation that gives minimum maternity and paternity leave for everyone employed. In the end, there is no 'right' time to start a family, but somehow those who do have made it work and perhaps made some trade-offs on career priorities.

Occasionally I have met students who ask about particular roles and industries in relation to starting families: 'But if I become a lawyer/consultant/teacher, when would I be able to have children?'

'When were you thinking of having children?' I ask the undergraduate.

'Oh, not for at least ten years!'

'Well, a lot can happen in ten years. For example, when we surveyed fifteen thousand alumni, they'd had an average of **three** different employers in the first ten years after leaving university. So you'll probably be with a different employer, maybe in a different industry, by the time you start thinking of planning families.'

The chart and rankings of ten features of a job are to start you thinking about what's important for you. And remember that this chart shows what undergraduates (roughly 18- to 22-year-olds) thought; at different ages, people have different priorities, so by the time you are 30, I'd guess that your priorities could be quite different.

## NOT A COMPETITION

The student was sitting across the table from me, in a Thursday morning one-to-one twenty-minute meeting.

'Could you look at my CV, please? I'm thinking of applying for management consultancy and want to send this off to a few firms this week.'

I scanned his CV; there was very little to suggest that his career path lay in management consultancy. I asked him, 'So, why are you thinking of consultancy?'

'All my friends are applying for consultancy; I'm not really sure what it is but it sounds fascinating.'

It can be difficult to remember that getting a job is not a competition with your friends as to who can get the better (whatever that means) job. And peer pressure can be very powerful in making any of us conform or follow a certain path; you've chosen your friends because you like them, you respect them, you admire some of their skills or characteristics, they make you feel good and you have an enjoyable time when you are with them – all of which means that you'll take note of when they've chosen to do something. While that can be a great indicator for recommendations about a new club, a recent movie, type of meal or holiday destination, it may not be the most useful indicator for how you're going to spend most of your waking hours for the next few years.

A further thought: you may think that all your friends are going into a specific type of job, but what does that mean? Are they just thinking about it? Applying? Signed an employment contract? And then there are some people who just want to be taking action and making applications.

'I've fallen behind my classmates,' said the thirty-year-old alumnus sitting before me.

'How do you know?' I asked.

'They are all earning at least £70K,' he answered.

'Is that your measure of success? What about intellectual challenge? Growing a business? Having choices? Making a difference?' I asked.

'No – none of those – I just want to get a new job that earns me more money.'

While I was taken aback by his attitude, perhaps I shouldn't have been. My research into what people want from a job (the summary chart is in the previous section) showed that there are two specific areas where men and women differ in terms of what they want: men seek 'High level of pay' much more than women do, and women seek 'A cause I feel good about, or serving the greater good' much more than men do. (When I say 'much more' I mean very statistically significantly, from a sample size of over 5000 sixth-formers and undergraduates.)

Remember at school when teachers told you that you were competing with yourself, not the others in the exam room? You may not have believed it then, but it really does apply here. Perhaps the moment you hear yourself saying, 'All my friends are going into . . .' is the moment to stop and ask how relevant that is to you. And recognise that you may have to be very strong to swim against the tide. In Part Two, there are some ideas of how you can reach out to other people who can help you think about the unusual course you have chosen, can tell you what the role is like and what it takes to succeed in applying and then in the job itself.

In the meantime, learn to steer your own course and not follow the boat in front – unless you really do want to end up where you think they think they're going.

## YOUR CAREER IS LIKE A SAILING TRIP

I once saw a famous Nobel Prize winner describe how he thought of his career as a sailing trip.

'The thing is,' he said, 'a career is a series of jobs that you have to tack between, to and fro, from one to another, beating against the wind to get where you want; you can't always go straight for the dock on the other side of the bay.'

I suppose I could extend the metaphor by saying that sometimes you get to run with the wind, when things are going in your favour, and other times the wind changes, the tide turns, a storm comes up, and you must trim your sails and change your plans.

He made a second point that can be really important to anyone just starting, or starting out after a break. 'You do have to actually put the sails up and leave the harbour; you can't just stay tied up thinking of all the many places that you could or might sail to.'

The other day we held an ice-breaker session for about sixty women students who were going to take part in our three-day holistic development course – everything from assertiveness to marketing yourself, and in all aspects of your life, not just academic work or career. Talking to the women about why they had chosen to come on the course (instead of going home for the holidays), several told me that they hoped it would provide some direction to their life, particularly because they felt there was 'so much choice on what to do'.

A graduate's parent told me at a dinner last month that her child was still not working since she was 'waiting for the perfect job'. As the Nobel Prize winner said, you do have to raise the sails and start the trip. There is no perfect job but getting started will help you find out what you like and help you get a better job. It is a truism that it is easier to get a job when you are already in a job; the potential, new employer can have some confidence that someone else has already employed you, and that you know about the world of work.

And for those waiting for the 'perfect' job, here's a spoiler alert: there is no such thing. However, this book will help you chart a course, set the sails, leave the harbour and get started, or make the change you want, so that you will get closer to a job that you'll enjoy, that will inspire you, and that will give you choices and control in life.

## OVERWHELMED BY CHOICE

There is such a thing as too much choice, and there is research that shows that when shoppers are presented with overwhelming choice, they choose not to make a decision at all. A well-known experiment in a supermarket by Mark Lepper and Sheena Iyengar appeared to show that when shoppers were offered a tasting array of twenty-four varieties of jam, only 3 per cent then went on to buy some with the money-off coupons they had been given, whereas when the tasting array was reduced to just six varieties, fully 30 per cent of shoppers bought some jam with their coupons. From this, they and others claimed that too much choice reduces actual decision-making.

To be fair, however, Benjamin Scheibehenne, a psychologist at the University of Basel, tried to repeat this experiment in a number of different ways and found no such association between amount of choice and preponderance of decision-making. Despite this, it is probably sensible to reduce choices somehow, especially if the sheer volume of choices is stopping you from moving on.

Barry Schwartz wrote about 'The Tyranny of Choice' in which he showed that too much choice can reduce overall happiness. He went on, with colleagues, to create a scale between those who he describes as *maximisers* and those who are *satisficers*. *Maximisers* aim to make the best possible choice, which means they have checked out every possibility and every option, comparing their choices with others' choices, and collecting and reading all the background research they can find. By contrast, *satisficers* settle for what they consider is good enough; they set targets and once they have found something that meets those targets they stop looking. One of the reasons that *maximisers* are less happy with their choices is, Schwartz states, the high opportunity cost of committing to one choice, and thereby excluding all those other possibilities, including of course, the ones yet to be identified.

### Wanting to check every possibility

I had spent the morning in a university department meeting students for fifteen-minute one-to-one discussions. My last appointment was a second-year engineer who wanted to apply for consulting. I asked him what work experience he had so far; he told me about his summer work at a major car company – as he did this, his eyes lit up, and he became very animated and excited about telling me all he had done.

'And, unusually, they've offered me a job next summer as well,' he finished.

> I probed a little. 'So why are you interested in applying for consulting when you've had, by your own description, such a wonderful experience *and* been offered another job next summer, and you know little about consulting?'
>
> He thought for a moment. 'I want to check that I'm getting the best job; even if I eventually join this car company, I want to know it was the best choice.'

By choosing one particular job over another (I interrupt to observe that we should all be so lucky to get more than one job offer . . .), or even choosing to explore opportunities in one sector over another, you will, inevitably, be closing some opportunities. Perhaps you've noticed in restaurants where there are few choices, or even no choices, it is so much easier and somehow more relaxing to choose, compared with restaurants with a long menu. Maybe that's partly why eating at a friend's house is relaxing as there is, usually, no choice of menu.

I digress; if you feel you are faced with the equivalent of a long menu of choices of what career to follow, then you will probably find it easier if you try to reduce the menu by adding some realism or stepping back to check what you are good at already and what you really enjoy doing. In Part Two, I'll explore how to do that in more detail, but for now recognise that you might be becoming paralysed by too much choice – the candy shop syndrome – and eventually must set off in one direction. How to get started – hoisting the sails on the yacht in the harbour – is next.

## GETTING STARTED

We've all faced it: the essay to write, the tax return to complete, the personal statement to draft, the project to design, the model to build, the field research to start – all characterised by the terrifying prospect of a real or metaphorical blank sheet of paper that you are expected to fill.

How to start? And why can this be difficult when you've done it before, and you know you have to do it – in fact there may be a looming deadline? Partly you may worry that you'll start wrongly and have to redo something later, or that you don't know how or where to start, or that something else is distracting you.

If we think about essays, you'll have learned that being able to edit drafts is really quite liberating – knowing that you can come back in five minutes or five days and rewrite something takes much of the pressure off you writing perfectly formed and beautiful English at the first attempt. Before computers, you might have drafted an essay and then rewritten the whole thing to incorporate your edits – now it can be much easier, as you can edit as you go along. You may also not get into the flow of your story/essay/project/model/research until you're a few paragraphs in.

A year after I started as a management consultant, one of the older partners observed that using computers made writing spreadsheets 'rather easy'; in 'his day' they had written spreadsheets by hand on large sheets of paper covered in gridlines. If they had forgotten a column or row, they either cut and glued extra paper in place, or erased whole sections – I think his message was that we should plan first before starting a spreadsheet. I disagree: the technology helps us just get started and learn by attempting the problem. This is clearly not always a good idea (flying a plane, surgery, travelling somewhere specific), but as a way not to be held up from even starting, it's great.

When I read students' cover letters, they usually start flowing well by the third paragraph after two rather stilted and generic paragraphs at the start. So perhaps one lesson to avoid prevarication is just to, well, start – knowing that you can come back and fix things later. One implication of this is that if you are just starting, you may not want to start with the most important job opportunity, but almost practise first on one that is not necessarily so important to you. In Part Two, when we come to discuss how to explore the sort of roles and industries that might interest you using Information Interviewing, we show that that method can help you polish your interviewing and research techniques in low pressure environments, before you need them to land you a job.

If you're held up because you don't know how to start, for example how to find people to talk to and set up an Information Interview, or how to refine your choices of jobs, then you could ask other people how they did it. Again, Part Two covers many of the practicalities of getting going.

As the Chinese philosopher Laozi (*c.* 604–531 BC) wrote, 'A journey of a thousand miles begins with the first step,' and while we hope your career map is not a thousand miles across, it still needs that critical first step, in almost any direction but getting some action and momentum.

## NOT A LIFE SENTENCE

The other week, in a one-to-one session, a student finally told me how worried he was about accepting the job offer that he had just received.

'I'm worried that if I accept this job, then I'll be stuck as an accountant (or teacher, or campaign manager) for all my life.'

A few weeks earlier, a student assured me: 'But my brother says that this job I take when I graduate is really important as I'll be doing it for ten or twenty years.'

And that same week, a student told me he didn't want to be 'locked into living in London for the next fifty years'.

When described like this, I'm sure you can see what I saw, and would have told all those students just how unlikely it would be for anyone to stay in the same job for five years, let alone forty. Perhaps their parents do, or more likely their grandparents did, have so-called jobs for life, but it has never been the case that you had to be in a job for life if you didn't want to and, on average, is getting even less true now.

I ran a survey of Oxford alumni about four years ago to ask them how many different employers they had had so far in their career, and how long they had been working. I asked them how long they had been working to try to take account of those who had taken time out from working, perhaps to start a family or to travel.

On average, the 15,000 alumni who completed the questionnaire had had **three different** employers in the first **ten** years of working. So that makes it about three to four years with each employer.

The rate of change seems to slow down: in the next ten years of working, the alumni's average is only one more different employer (that is, four different employers in the first twenty years). Perhaps this is because people had found what they like to do, or where they like to live, or they have started to have partners and families that make it more difficult to move, or some combination of all of these.

I also asked the alumni in which industries they had worked, to see if some industries were 'stickier' than others. The average of three employers in the first ten years is, indeed, just an average, and masks a range of around two different employers (for lawyers) up to about five different employers (for those in social care, or hospitality and tourism). The chart below shows the full range.

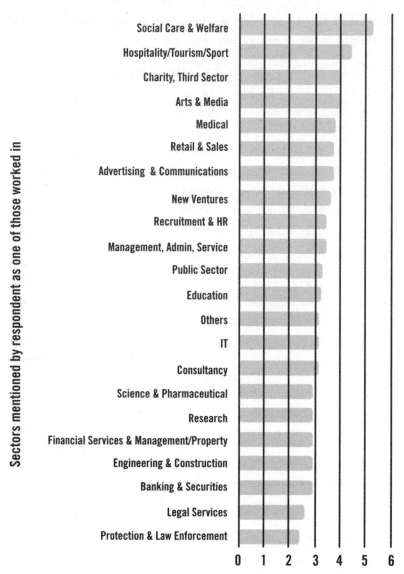

Graph shows number of sectors worked in, in the first ten
years of working after leaving Oxford (n=15,000)

I analysed which other sectors people said they had worked in (is it
true that 'once a teacher, always a teacher'?) and found that people
had moved about quite considerably. Lawyers and doctors had

WHERE AM I GOING AND CAN I HAVE A MAP?

worked in about one other sector, while those in social care had worked in three other sectors.

The median age of the respondents to my survey was thirty-eight, and many commentators would say that the workforce is getting more mobile. The *millennials* (that is, those born between about 1982 and 2000) may not stay in jobs for as long as those in this survey, seeking more experiences in life. In other words, for today's students and recent graduates, the number of different employers in the first ten years is probably going to be higher than three and, therefore, the time spent with each employer will be less than three years.

None of this means that you will *have* to move jobs every two to three years; it can be just as strong a decision to stay with an employer or in a particular job because it's going well, rather than jumping off just because you've been there a certain time. But this should reassure those students I mentioned at the start, that by taking a job, they'd be very unusual if they then stayed more than three, four or even five years initially.

## ONLY HERE ONCE
While some people believe in reincarnation, even they don't generally believe that you will be reborn in the same form or able to have a second chance at the type of life you are leading now. Therefore, if we are only here in this form once, it's worth taking some care on how to spend the time. How many people have you heard say, 'If I had my time again, I would . . .'?

Well, your time is now, and if you want to change some or all of it, then don't wait. There may only be some aspects of your life that are frustrating you and can be fixed, without throwing everything out.

A few months ago an early career researcher who worked in a scientific laboratory came to an afternoon session based on the psychological profiling known as MBTI®. She was feeling frustrated with her work and what she considered excessive time at the lab bench. She had evidently carved out what appeared to be a successful career and was trying to combine this with a family life, including young children. Her MBTI profile showed that her preferred style was to work at a more strategic and intuitive level, rather than in a detailed, operational way. Armed with this insight, she reflected at the end of the session that she could make a large and positive difference to her life, if she could reduce the time spent at the lab bench and spend that time on the strategic issues of the work. She left the session with a clear plan of what she would talk to her boss about the next day.

### MBTI® (Myers-Briggs Type Indicator)

Based on Carl Jung's philosophy that human beings experience the world through four key functions – sensation, intuition, feeling and thinking – and that the preferences we have for these don't change with age, the MBTI test sets out to measure how strongly you experience the world on each of these functions as a way to give you insight on your preferred thinking and working style.

You may have had a similar profile run for you; while the MBTI® programme takes a couple of hours and has to be administered by a trained practitioner, you can try a simplified version on the icould. com website.

If you are compromising one or more aspects of your current role, be really clear why you are doing it. You may decide not to take the promotion or new role in another city so you can remain with your partner or near an ageing relative; alternatively, you may decide that you have to leave the well-paid role and seek a lower paid but more interesting job in another location so that you can be near a relative, or be in an area where you can play the sport or hobby you enjoy.

Most of the time, we are all making a compromise – but so long as you are clear what that compromise is and that it is still worth it, or even still necessary, then carry on. As I'll discuss in the section on negotiation, it can be powerful to challenge whether aspects that you consider fixed are, in fact, variable. Do you really need to be in this city? This industry? Near this school? This close to or far from your work? This dependent on your car? In this size house or flat? It can be liberating to challenge every aspect of your current life – even if you feel the ground move under your feet – you'll be surprised (I hope) how many of the aspects are, in fact, fine and that you have alighted on the best position for you.

If you think about it, we are all effectively volunteers for work, so make sure you want to get out of bed to do that work. It may not be easy to make changes, and it may take some time – perhaps years if you, for example, set out to get a new qualification while needing to have an income from what you feel is a 'dead-end' job to keep food on the table. But armed with that plan, and strong ambition to make the change, you won't be one of those saying, 'If I had my time over again . . .'

## WHAT'S THE AIM?
## (HINT, IT'S NOT THE MONEY)

If you want one overarching goal for your life and career, it seems that what makes most of us happy and content is to have choice and control in our career, doing something we personally consider worthwhile. If others value what you do, they will demonstrate this, usually by paying you, but also by giving you recognition. What you think is 'worthwhile' is different for everyone – and we'll explore that in Part Two.

Careers and jobs are a means to the end of fulfilling your needs; Maslow's 'Hierarchy of Needs' can point the way. At its most basic, a job enables you to have somewhere to live and to be able to feed, wash and clothe yourself. Beyond that, jobs and careers can provide financial security, friendship, recognition and the ability to master an important skill or develop a recognised expertise.

### Hierarchy of Needs

Abraham Maslow proposed a famous hierarchy of needs, in a seminal paper of 1943, 'A Theory of Human Motivation'. He proposed five layers, each of which humans seek to fulfil before being able to move to the next; in ascending order of importance they are:

★ Physiological – shelter, food, heat, clothing
★ Safety – personal and financial security, health and well-being
★ Love/belonging – friendship, intimacy and family
★ Esteem – recognition, fame, respect, prestige, attention
★ Self-actualisation – 'to achieve all one can be, to achieve mastery of specific skills'

Of course, to begin with you will have less choice and control – even if you decide to be self-employed (or are in a job that is by definition self-employed, for example, being a barrister). So that you ultimately have control and choice, you will actually have given quite a lot of control to your customers or clients.

As you consider your next move, or promotion, you can think about whether it will increase your options, give you more choice over the next few years, or narrow down your choices. Will it add more skills or experiences that will fit, like another jigsaw piece, into the picture of your career?

And then we have the question whether you consider the job 'worthwhile'. Just after I started my current job, a student reporter from one of the student newspapers rang me to ask for information on an article he was writing.

'What is the job that will do the most good in the world?' he asked.

I answered, 'Investment banker.'

'No, that's not right,' he said. 'It can't be that.'

'Well, how about actor, night-club singer, teacher or oil exploration engineer?'

'Some of those are better,' he said, perhaps with a dawning realisation that there is no answer to the question. Like all good essay questions, the first response is really: it depends what you mean by 'good'.

I could make a case for each of the example jobs above doing the most good in the world, but for you to agree, it would depend on you sharing my values and measures of 'good'.

Two years ago, a female engineering student came to one of my one-to-one sessions. She started the session by telling me:

'I've found a fabulous graduate programme with Rolls-Royce, but I don't want to work on military-related equipment, only on civilian aircraft, and thought I'd tell them that as part of my application.'

'If you put yourself in their position,' I asked, 'how do you think they will treat your application?'

'Hmm, I see. It may be difficult for them to separate the work, as the same jet engine could be used in a search and rescue helicopter as in a fighter aircraft.'

We discussed other options, including her working with 'Engineers without Borders', so that she could apply her skills and expertise in an environment that she personally would find worthwhile. At this stage, it can help narrow down your choices if you define what you consider 'worthwhile'.

## TAKE CHARGE OF YOUR OWN CAREER

Is your career a thing or concept that is separate from you? Are you defined by your role? Is a career something that just happens to you – and is it basically a stream of jobs? Is anyone in charge of your career? Who actually cares, long-term, about what job you take and what direction your career takes? If other people do care, then do you agree with their choices?

There are people and institutions around to help you and suggest careers and jobs for you, there are computer programs and books that will suggest specific directions based on you answering a few dozen questions, and there are friends and family who tell you what they think is best. In the end, it's pretty much down to you to take charge of your own life. As the character Iris Simpkins (played by Kate Winslet) says in the 2012 film *The Holiday* (part set in the Hollywood movie industry), 'You're supposed to be the leading lady of your own life.' Or leading man, of course.

There has been a trend for the classic signs of adulthood to occur five to ten years later than they did forty years ago; instead of people getting married, moving out of the family home, becoming financially independent, finishing education and starting families in their early to mid twenties, it's now late twenties to early thirties. While marriage has been seen by anthropologists as a key transition point in becoming an adult, research by Peter Arnett, published in 1998, reported that when given a choice of thirty-eight different measures of 'adulthood', fully 94 per cent of 140 young Americans cited 'Accept responsibility for the consequences of your actions' as the leading characteristic of being an adult (marriage was ranked no. 31, supported by only 17 per cent).

As you progressed through school and university you had increasingly more control of your timetable, your choices, and how you spent each day. While the blank timetable of work beyond university, or beyond this current job, can be scary, you do at least want to be the one to write out the plans, rather than letting others fill in the blank sheet.

By contrast, the annual survey of hundreds of thousands of students across the world, the Student Barometer, consistently reports that about 20 per cent of international students studying in the UK 'expect their university to find them a job'. This could be done; however, I'd suggest there are two good reasons why this is not ideal. First, the students probably wouldn't like the job the university found them, and second, the university probably doesn't welcome the idea of being wholly responsible for someone's future happiness and career.

If you rely on others to have a plan for your career, you may be surprised to find that, well, they don't have that much actually planned for you. Take charge and become the leading man or woman in your own life, seek advice to help you take responsibility, and remember that you don't have to take the advice you're given.

## WOULD YOU LIKE THE TRUTH?

A second-year historian sat opposite me, wanting to rehearse some questions for an interview he had the following week. I started with what can be the easiest and yet most telling question of all: easiest, because you can and should prepare your answer, and most telling, because it goes to the heart of why you are sitting there, at the interview.

'What attracted you to this job?'

There was a pause, and then he said, in all seriousness, 'Would you like the honest answer?'

I have to admit that this response was not what I was expecting. It's not that I was expecting a fully formed, perfect set of three reasons why he was attracted to the job, how it played to his skills, how the organisation was supportive and inspiring, and what he could bring to the role, but I was expecting some attempt at it.

'Let's try the honest answer,' I said, 'and see what it's like.'

'Well, I've tried other jobs, in other organisations, and realised they weren't for me. Friends I've spoken to who have worked at this place are really positive about it.'

As it happened, the 'honest answer' was excellent, and had the added bonus of being the truth. One problem with being dishonest (leaving ethics aside for a moment) is to remember the false story correctly. If you have secured a job using a somewhat false story (for example, around your motives for wanting the job) then you are going to have to stick to that story and, in a job, actually live that story, day in, day out.

Just after I started my current job, I visited a leading investment bank. As part of my visit, a recent biochemistry graduate showed me around the trading floors; after about twenty minutes, and in a deserted stairwell, she confided in me that she had been there fifteen months and was going to leave the moment her bonus came through, so that she could move to a job using her biochemistry. While she had been attracted to the bank initially, she realised she had not been honest with herself as to what she really wanted to do. Perhaps she had needed to take the job to find this out by actually doing the job, maybe she had been swept along with her peers and been flattered to be offered the highly prestigious role. As it happened, events overtook her; three months later, the bank declared bankruptcy and her job disappeared.

One of the personal attributes interviewers and recruiters are looking for is honesty or integrity – can they trust you? Obviously they aren't going to ask that question directly – how might the interview go?

'Are you honest?'

There's only one acceptable answer in this situation: 'Yes.'

However, a more honest answer might be to deconstruct the question; in what situation, at what level, to what end? The parent who told their child that ice cream vans ring their chimes when they are empty of ice cream may have had perfectly good motives but was not being exactly honest.

Instead, interviewers will assess your integrity by your overall approach, your consistency, your openness to discussing difficulties, mistakes, gaps in your CV and so on. As I'll discuss later, interviewers are essentially deciding if they could work with you: do you take responsibility, achieve things and would you fit within the team? Honesty, integrity, and openness are key to that fit; conversely, if they were looking for someone who is not always honest, then perhaps you wouldn't want to work in that culture.

## IT'S A LONG GAME

It is perhaps a sobering thought that for people in their twenties, careers are going to last up to fifty years. Of course, on the 'glass half empty or glass half full' argument* you might think that you'll need fifty years to try everything you'd quite like to do.

*As an engineer, my view is that the glass was designed to be twice as big as it needed to be.

Today, the life expectancy of a twenty-year-old is around eighty years in the Western world; in 1900 it was around sixty-five years. And the quality of that life, with better diets, healthcare and overall fitness levels, means that, in principle, people will be able to continue working until they are seventy or more, if they want or (given most people's pension planning) have to. The model of a few years of retirement, to get one's affairs in order, used by Bismarck when he introduced pensions, was based around a life expectancy of the biblical three score years and ten (that is, seventy in total) – hence a retirement age of sixty or sixty-five.

Even though I wrote earlier that you should take some care to make sure you are in a job that is serving most of your overall values and aims, it doesn't hurt to stick at something for a few years – in fact, sometimes the real value of understanding, or of making significant changes, can only come about with the passage of time.

### Working the railways

A few years ago, I visited the Swindon Railway Museum, and it happened to be a day when some retired train drivers were by the exhibits, talking to visitors about what it was like to drive the locomotives, shovel the coal, work the signal boxes and so on.

One train driver explained to me the extensive period of his training: the first two years he was only allowed to drive a loco in the shunting yard, then he progressed to be a fireman on the branch and main lines, and only after ten years or so, did he progress to driving a passenger train. One of the benefits, in his mind, was that he could drive a laden passenger train by hearing the line – he could tell, from his experience, where he was on every part of the 140-mile London–Swansea line just by the sounds of the line and the echoes. He described how useful this could be in thick fog or at night.

WHERE AM I GOING AND CAN I HAVE A MAP?

Perhaps modern trains with modern signalling don't need to rely on this human experience, but it did bring an added layer of safety and, it seemed, enhanced job satisfaction and teamwork.

It's not essential to keep moving every two to three years – and there are some significant benefits of staying in the same organisation, and even the same role, for a year or more. If you do decide to seek a new role in the same organisation, perhaps promotion to managing the team you are currently in, then there's a whole other set of issues I cover in the Internal Promotion section. While there are difficulties to overcome, the benefits include working with people you already know, in an organisation and culture with which you are familiar.

It's a continuous balancing act: could you do better by moving, or going for internal promotion versus making more out of your current role? Are you stagnating in your current job and feel you are settling into a comfortable rut, versus the disruption and perhaps frightening challenge of exploring what you'd really want to do that might necessitate change?

In the next section, I'll explore the possible invisible forces that might be acting on you in this balancing act – like winds blowing a tightrope walker – and you'll at least be able to name them and decide how important each of them is to you.

## WHAT INVISIBLE FORCES ARE ACTING ON YOU?

Invisible forces such as gravity and magnetism shape our world; there are other forces that also operate on each of us, sometimes independently from any human agency, and some of these have been the subject of religious and philosophical thought through the ages. These include: internal biological forces, dreams, beliefs, laws, social attitudes, cultural rules, peer pressure, and strong emotions, such as fear and anger.

As far as your career is concerned, these invisible forces will exert influence on you, limit your choices and encourage you in certain directions. You probably had little control over the school you went to or where you grew up – it's difficult to argue successfully at the age of five about which primary school you'd like to attend, or to leave home at thirteen because you'd rather live in another town. By sixth form, you'll have been more successful in choosing the subjects you wanted to study, or selecting the apprenticeship you wanted to go on; in theory, or ideally, your parents will have been trusting you more and beginning to realise that you had your own life with your own choices to make.

Selecting your university, college, apprenticeship or place of work will have been much more your choice, though you will have been subject to external, invisible forces such as peer pressure, parental influence, social attitudes, anxiety, and beliefs.

As you set out on the next step in your career pathway, it's going to be important and helpful to understand the constraints and invisible forces acting on you, and to challenge each one. Anecdotally, I would observe that most students I meet will explicitly mention these invisible forces, for example: 'My friends are . . ', or 'My tutor suggests . . ', or 'This is a well-respected organisation . . ', or 'I don't want to enter this industry/sector as it doesn't support my personal values . . ', or 'It pays well . . ', or 'I want to work in London . . '.

## Breaking family ties

Sometimes the invisible force can be very strong, long-term and highly emotional. A Muslim woman student came to one of my one-to-one sessions a few years ago to ask for career advice around applying for a Masters degree. She was the first in her family to come to university.

'Are your family very proud of you to be at Oxford?' I asked at the end of our meeting.

'Not at all,' was her unexpected response. 'Above all, my mother wanted me to be married. I've had to effectively break away from home to follow this path.'

If you find yourself saying phrases like this, or having what you consider is too narrow a range of jobs to apply for, then you could list all the invisible forces and how each is constraining or driving you. You may yet decide that these forces and their influence are immutable – for example, you may not wish or feel you are able to change strongly held values or religious beliefs – but at least you would have identified and defined these forces, and understood how they are setting some limits or imposing some direction on your choices.

Here's an idea for a structured way to identify and review these external forces: to name them, define each one, assess the strength of each force, identify how that force is constraining you and in what direction it is pushing you. For example:

| Force | Definition | Strength | Constraint or Driver |
| --- | --- | --- | --- |
| Social values | To help those less well off than me | Strong – primary importance to me; essential for any role to be centred on this | Focus on social enterprises, charities, teaching in deprived areas |

Now, here's an expanded table – you should create your own list of forces and your own way to explain strengths (for example, 'essential', 'important', and 'nice to have') and for each one, whether the focus is the constraining or driving factor.

| Force | Definition | Strength | Constraint or Driver |
|---|---|---|---|
| Location | | | |
| Beliefs | | | |
| Values | | | |
| Income/pay | | | |
| Peer pressure | | | |
| Family / partner | | | |
| Financial | | | |
| Health | | | |
| Ambition | | | |

Having identified invisible forces that might be constraining your career choices, feel free to challenge them: how strong are they? Just how constraining, if at all? For example, if you think you are being constrained to certain locations by your parents, partners, or children, then talk to them to understand what they want.

You might be pleasantly surprised. You might learn that they'd quite like to move to another city/country, perhaps you can persuade them to consider a change, perhaps they're thinking of moving anyway and were waiting for you? Also, remember that they might need some time to absorb your plans and suggestions, so don't take their first answer for a final answer.

The table of invisible forces is a checklist for your negotiation with yourself and, like the best negotiators, you will see how you can change fixed items into variable factors; you may also get the help of a negotiation adviser – a friend, or an impartial adviser (tutor, careers adviser, personal mentor) – who can challenge you and help you explore changes you may not have spotted. Armed with your checklist, you have already started to plan – and there is much more detailed help in Part Two. First, though, there is a balance to be struck on how much planning is helpful, and I'll cover that next, as the last part of this section.

## PLANNING AND OVERPLANNING

I had been describing to a third-year student the idea that he didn't need to feel he was locked into a job for ten years, but could, if he so chose, leave after a couple of years – and, in fact, that was the average for leavers from Oxford.

'But I want to make sure I'm not wasting any time in a job,' he commented, 'and not just the first job but each one.'

'Am I right in thinking that you want your career all planned out? You want to make sure each role isn't wasted and builds on the previous roles?' I asked.

'Yes, that's right. All planned out.'

I checked his position a little. 'You mean until you retire? The next forty or fifty years?'

'Yes, then I'll know my career is well planned and I won't be wasting time.'

I'm not sure that this student was so unusual, even if he was maybe a little extreme. It can be good to have a rough direction of travel across the map in mind, even if it's only how the ideal job would feel, or it can be positively challenging to set yourself a goal of an ideal job three years out, even if you can't see the steps between now and then. But to hope to plan in detail thirty, twenty or even ten years into the future is setting a very high expectation and one with a low chance of accurate success.

I talked to the student about the way that life has a way of turning things up that the best plans do not anticipate. On the positive side that may include love, new technologies, job opportunities, children; and on the immediately negative side, organisations downsizing so you lose your job through no fault of your own, changes to the national economy, personal health issues, and family pressures.

There has been a tendency for some students to develop a long-term plan, in probably unachievable levels of detail and to set up detailed targets that may constrain or become irrelevant.

## We chose to go to the moon

Perhaps one of the most famous ten-year plans was declared in 1961 in speeches by President John F. Kennedy, first to the US Congress, and later at an open-air speech at Rice University, Texas.

He set an incredibly ambitious target – to send a man to the moon and bring him back safely, by the end of the decade. In those speeches, Kennedy did not lay out the details of the plan, though he acknowledged the overall costs involved and that some 'other things' would need to be sorted – in this case, the minor details of the (unproven) Saturn V launch rocket.

Your career plan can start from a moon ambition – 'In ten years, I want to be a senior manager/professor/doctor/charity founder working in the area of climate change/disaster relief/nuclear fusion/Shakespeare's plays.' And then a plan for the first year or two can start from there; though you wouldn't try to plan the whole ten years, as there are just too many unknowns in three to five years' time.

Another student was talking to me about various industry sectors she had been considering.

'I'm not going to apply for that industry, because when would I have a family?'

'An interesting overall concern and, if you're planning to have children, it is indeed something you may wish to take into account. When, if I may ask, are you thinking of having children?'

She answered, 'Oh not for years, I don't even have a partner at the moment.'

I suggested that she might want to reduce the relative importance of this issue of finding a family-friendly employer. 'After all, there are many unknowns here: your partner and their career, the employer, legislation in several years' time, employer attitudes, and then even when that's all settled, women don't always get pregnant when they plan to. So my advice is not to overthink this – keep a weather eye open on the issue.'

In an unchanging world and armed with perfect knowledge about yourself, all employers, jobs, economies and other candidates, you'd be able to set a plan and execute exactly that plan for your entire career. Even if that were possible, where would be the fun in having your whole career planned out for the next fifty years?

Note I wrote, 'unchanging world', which includes you, and means that you won't change either; perhaps you think that's possible – at the tender age of eighteen or twenty-one or thirty, have you finished developing? But why, at this precise moment, have you stopped changing, developing, learning new skills, adding more experiences, making new friends and so on?

I've probably overdone this argument and I hope made the point that you, jobs, employers, roles, products, services, economies and the environment are all changing – not so fast that you can't keep up, but enough so that, on the one hand, you can't rely on an unchanging career and, on the other hand, that new and interesting opportunities will come up next week, next month and next year.

As Robert Burns wrote, 'The best-laid schemes o' mice an' men / gang aft agley [go often awry]'. In terms of your career map, I think this means don't try to see the whole map, from today to the end of your career, but fill in the details of the part of the map nearest you, then leave the parts that are further away, to be sketched in roughly. As you travel across your map, the distant parts will get more detailed as they come closer, like on a SatNav, even if you can't see them very clearly yet.

In Part Two, I'll describe some practical tools for career map reading, and answer the question, 'What do I do on Monday morning?'

......................

# Practicalities, or what do I do on Monday morning?

......................

## DOWN TO GROUND LEVEL

In Part One, I suggested you were in a helicopter, at 10,000 feet above your map, so you could see the big picture and understand where you were heading in the next one, five, or ten years. You thought about the invisible forces acting on you, the idea that there is no 'right' answer to your career, you're not in competition and, while you can't plan in too much detail, you could do with a rough and even ambitious long-term target.

So far, so theoretical.

In Part Two, you land the helicopter at the start of the map, with an overall direction in mind and a yearning to start the trek. This section is all about 'How to': How to find a job, How to write a great application, How to meet people and How to get their help, How to interview to show you at your best, How to negotiate the offer, and more besides.

## WAYS TO FIND A JOB

Last term, a student asked me, 'What's the most efficient way to find a job? I don't want to waste any time on ways that don't work.'

Looking for a job can, of course, lead down some blind alleys – for example, you apply but don't get asked for interview, or you decide not to take the job they offer you, or you talk to people about jobs and industries that you decide you don't want to follow up – is this wasted time? Some of it may be, but not all of it, and anyway, it's in the past and was probably unavoidable. And there are some people (the maximisers in Part One) who will think if they get the first job they apply for, that maybe there was a better one that they hadn't found yet.

But to answer the question another way, there are six main ways to find a job: it's worth thinking about each one and knowing which ones you are going to use and when, how much effort to put into each, and which might be more or less successful depending on what stage you are at in your career and on what sort of job you want.

As a caveat, this discussion is really about professional jobs so is not so applicable to temporary or seasonal work such as in cafés or bars. That's not to say that seasonal, temporary work isn't valuable – it can show future employers many good skills, and we'll cover that elsewhere; but for this section, we'll focus on (for want of a better term) professional or graduate-level work.

In no particular order, the six ways are: answering a job ad, cold calling, networking, executive search, creating your own job, and getting promoted from your current job. I'll discuss each of these, at the end of which you'll be able to decide which route or routes to follow and how much effort to put into each one. Let's start with probably the most apparent and one that most people spend a lot of time on to begin with: answering a job ad.

### Answering a job ad

Undoubtedly the most obvious way to find a job is to look at the ads, whether in the newspapers or, much more likely, on websites. An ad gives you an instant window on the job, the key details such as job title, salary, location and employer; you can scan dozens of them very quickly, whether in print or online.

You can register your interest and receive alerts when online jobs that appear to match your choices are posted. Anyone who has registered finds that they are quickly overwhelmed with email alerts about jobs, most of which are of little interest – it can be difficult to spot the ones that you really want.

An ad (and the job description behind the ad) tells you about the role, confirms that the organisation is actually intending to recruit and has one or more vacancies, when they would want you to start, and how much they'll pay (for most jobs – some of them just say 'competitive salary'). They'll also explain how they are going to choose by listing some Selection Criteria, some of which will be Essential and some Desirable. Just the action of placing an ad shows you that the company has spent money (perhaps) and time and effort (definitely) on writing the ad and uploading it – so to that extent, they are probably serious. The ad will also have a call to action: you'll be able to download more information on the job, including exactly how to apply, with what documents, and by when. We'll cover all of that later in this section.

On the flip side, many other people apart from you will also have seen the ad and will be thinking of applying. Companies regularly tell me that they get about 10,000 applicants for 100 places on their graduate scheme. This is not to put you off, just to say that there's an element of a numbers game here.

One recruiter told me, 'When I get hundreds of great looking applications, I print them out, take them to the top of the stairs and throw them down. Those that land face up go on to the next stage, the rest are rejected.'

That may be an exaggeration (and I do hope so) but it makes the point that for really popular roles your perfect application may be rejected for a really random reason.

The point of this is, I suppose, to show that once you have chosen to apply, you are no longer in control of the process; you end up metaphorically sitting by the phone waiting for the call. While answering ads can form part of any combined approach, and may even be a necessary part of a process that you have uncovered through one of the other routes below, it shouldn't be your only route. The next two put you in control of your job search; having more control usually makes people happier.

## Cold calling

When I was leaving the consulting company I worked for in San Francisco, I had a colleague who, I learned later, was also planning on leaving. He had a different job-hunting approach to mine: he was extremely keen to work for one particular hi-tech company in Silicon Valley. The problem was that they weren't advertising any jobs at that time.

'Never mind that,' he told me. 'I decided to write to every vice-president and ask for a short meeting.' Since there were about a dozen vice-presidents, looking after sales, marketing, production, finance, design and so on, it seemed like he had had a few letters to write. After two or three attempts, with an initial letter (this was all pre-Internet), and two or three follow-up phone calls, he had achieved just one lunch meeting with one vice-president – but it was at the company where he really wanted to work.

After that one lunch, his host had passed his details to one of her colleagues, and he had eventually received another invitation to a meeting with that colleague who worked in the department he was interested in. This is not meant to be a fairy story, but as a result of all his focused hard work, he did get a job in his target hi-tech company.

So my second method of finding a job, cold calling, can work; in preparation, you will have done immense research and developed some burning ambition as to why this particular organisation – and you will be able to articulate: Why them? Perhaps it's the products or services, the culture, or the people – in ten seconds you'll need to be able to answer, 'Why us?'

You'll also have some really in-depth knowledge about the organisation, and perhaps the specific area you want to work in; and then you'll need persistence and energy. One way you'll be able to collect this information is through networking – so we'll cover that next.

## Networking

It is said that 'the majority of jobs are never advertised'. I don't have the evidence for that 'fact' but clearly there must be at least some jobs that are not seen openly, or perhaps don't exist until someone suggests they could do the (then non-existent) job. Sometimes there's a chicken and egg effect: meeting someone prompts the employer to think, 'You know what, that person is really talented and could do this project we've been thinking about for some time.' At this point, you become the only candidate for the project – a pretty good position to be in.

How to network or hold Information Interviews are covered in other sections so I won't repeat them here – suffice it to say here that getting out and about and meeting people is a great way to learn about work, industries, organisations and opportunities; and it can be a way to generate opportunities – making your own luck.

Whether you're going to try cold calling a specific organisation you'd like to work in, or just want to explore your options (Is the grass really greener in another organisation? Why are all my friends applying for jobs in a particular sector?), you'll want to collect some information, and in so doing, you'll want to build a network – the third method of finding a job.

You already have a network – even if today most of it is with people you knew or know from school and college, and it's all about their holidays, their views about a TV series, or pictures of their cat that can stand on its back legs. The networking I'm suggesting here is, shall we say, more professional although some of your friends from your social network should also be in your professional network. You'll probably start to add in other people to your professional network including: people you meet, your tutors, someone you worked for during work experience, contacts from your parents and your friends' parents.

One way to build a network today is using professional networking Internet sites such as LinkedIn. You can start building your network with people you know or via contacts including from family, tutors, and work; you can then expand the network by reaching out to second- or third-degree connections who work in organisations or industries you are interested in. Once you've registered on LinkedIn, you can reach people directly; even if you are not registered you can still search for people who were at your school or college, worked in a specific organisation, or have listed interests in something you care about.

You can also neatly keep your social and professional networks separate using Facebook or similar for the former, and LinkedIn or similar for the latter. Might be worth mentioning here that employers or people you are trying to connect with can potentially read your Facebook profile – so clean up your information and check your security settings. People who might be reading your LinkedIn profile are so-called *headhunters* – or more accurately executive search – so they are up next.

### Executive search

The fourth way to get a new job is for the job to come to you – via an executive search firm. You're sitting at work, concentrating hard on a task, when the phone rings. 'Hello, it's Mary Smith from XYZ Search here. We're managing the search for the International Widget Corporation to find their new Sales Director and I was wondering if you could suggest anyone?'

International Widget has clearly decided that the role is so senior or so difficult to fill that they have employed a firm to conduct the search, and they are prepared to pay XYZ Search around 30 per cent of the starting salary of the new person as the finder's fee. XYZ Search will have a database of people they have met and now they are reaching out to other people who could help them in their search. You will be a successful sales manager and someone will have suggested your name to them.

Their real question is whether *you* would be interested – and, at the end of the conversation about other people you could suggest, Mary Smith will very likely ask if perhaps you might be interested.

While executive search can undoubtedly be a great way to get a new job, it is not in your control as the job seeker when the phone will ring. In addition, when you are a new graduate or just starting your career, it is unlikely that you will be of much interest for the type and level of jobs that executive search are hired to fill. Finally, it is important to remember that Mary Smith is working not for you, but for International Widget.

Having said that, it can be worth meeting some executive search staff, to get registered on their databases and to start to become known. They may give you a few minutes and will definitely keep your details on their database – who knows, a relevant search and opportunity may arise and it would be a shame if they didn't know about you. Many of them specialise by sector, for example Fundraising or Computer programming skills – so if you do want to register on their books, then seek out the most appropriate firm(s).

## Create your own job

As the old joke goes, if there's no light at the end of the tunnel, go and switch it on yourself, in this case by being self-employed, or working for yourself. You could also include starting your own business – perhaps with just you as the only employee to start with, but once it starts being successful, you might bring in others to work with you or for you. It can be very rewarding – you are your own boss, able to work when you want, and you can pick and choose who you work with and on what projects. That's the theory of course; in reality, you may not have much choice on who you work with, where they are and what the work is; it's difficult to switch off from making the business grow; it can be lonely (no colleagues to chat to about projects or even last night's TV); you have to do everything from ordering the stationery to marketing to clients; and it's hard work with long hours.

Depending on what you want to do, you'll probably have more choice if you have some specific skills or experiences that customers want: this may be bricklaying or foreign language translation, gardening or website coding. You may also find some experiences of 'business' to be helpful; so if you haven't got this, seek out a course at the local university, council or college to get the basics. You may also choose to take a job in a business for a few years to understand what your future customers want and how they operate. Unlike individuals, companies can take a long time to decide to buy a service, may have even longer processes to choose who they want to do the service, and take even longer still to pay. It's worth knowing about this before you decide to go it alone.

And while there's great emphasis these days on 'entrepreneurship', with courses at schools, colleges and universities, and with programmes like *Dragons' Den* and *The Apprentice,* the skills and ability to be *innovative* are valued by *all* employers. If you develop some entrepreneurial skills, you may well start your career in a large organisation and then, after several years, strike out on your own.

## Internal promotion

Sixth, and finally, the easiest job to get is the one you already have, and perhaps the next easiest job to get is to be promoted. But it can also be very difficult to get a new job in your current organisation because they know you so well. So when a new post, let's say above your current position in the organisation, is advertised or even just talked about, what should you do?

First, I'd suggest you think about whether you actually want the job – perhaps there's already a formal job description you can read, or you can talk to the person to whom the new job will report. Second, if you've decided you want to apply, I'd go and talk to your current boss and the people likely to be involved in the appointment. Here you're listening out for verbal cues, such as, 'I'd really encourage you to apply', or 'You'd be really good at this'. If you hear these lines, then you can give it serious consideration.

If, however, you hear lines like, 'By all means, throw your hat in the ring', or 'We'd be interested in your application', or 'Well, I can't obviously promise anything and it is an open competition', then you should be much more circumspect about whether to invest any more time.

Of course, it should be an open competition; you want to win the job fair and square so that your future colleagues will respect you and not undermine you with mutterings and rumour about how you got the job.

Your next challenge, once you decide to apply, is to level the playing field with external candidates. Clearly, the interviewers know you better than outsiders, though it will help you if the interview panel includes an external member who does not know you. The most important thing to remember, as an applicant, is to treat all the interviewers as new to you, and as people who do *not* know you. In other words, don't assume that they know all about your projects and work that you have done for them; even if they do know, it does no harm to remind them. As you complete the application form, letter or during the interview, avoid the following:

Interviewer: 'Can you tell us about a time when you ran a project successfully?'

You: 'Well, you know the project I did for you last year? That went well, didn't it?'

Better to treat the interviewer as someone who does not know about the project, and answer the question fully (for example, using the STAR technique I describe in the Interview section). If there are external people on the interview panel, make sure you spell out any jargon or acronyms that you use internally.

And, of course, the people interviewing you who you have worked with will know and remember your mistakes and weaknesses, so don't try to cover those up; think hard about how you will explain them, without dwelling on them, and how you have reflected and learned from them.

That's six different ways to find a job; whichever route(s) you go down, the next step is to define what you are looking for.

## WHAT DO YOU WANT?

Last year, I met a chemistry student who said, 'I've been applying for quite a few jobs, but I'm not sure I really want any of them.'

I asked her, 'Why those particular jobs?'

To which she replied, 'I don't know really; they looked like they might be interesting, they are well known organisations, and I'd be using my subject.'

We discussed this. 'It seems to me,' I suggested, 'it's as though you've gone to the lab, mixed up some random chemicals that sound interesting, in the hope that you'll get some result – though you're not sure what. Consequently, you haven't got anything interesting, despite considerable activity and energy. Wouldn't you normally plan a chemical experiment before getting to the practical stage?'

**Target practice**

If you don't have a target or objective, then I assume you won't mind where you end up. While that might look like giving you an infinite number of options, it's unlikely that you're such a blank sheet of paper that you'll be good at anything and enjoy everything.

About a third of students I meet confess (for sometimes it feels like it's a confession) that they have no idea what career or job they want. If you feel like this, then you're in good company. If the longest journey begins with the first step, then your first step here is to think about what is important to you, what you care about. Some answers I've heard include: earning enough money, doing something worthwhile, making people happy, helping others, producing real things, leaving the world a better place, researching new ideas or things, and teaching people new skills. It can also include a list of what is not important to you; examples I've heard include: earning lots of money, doing academic research, teaching, starting up a new company and so on.

Have a look back at the chart at the beginning of Part One showing the ten features of a job and how one group of 850 students prioritised them.

It can help if you reflect on what you've enjoyed doing in the past, perhaps at school – what societies and hobbies you've taken on, what sport, music, drama you've been involved in – and within those activities, what *particular* features you've enjoyed. Did you like the intellectual challenge? The underlying cause you were serving? Managing the technical side of drama? Acting centre stage? Leading a team? Starting a new activity and inspiring others to join in? Or developing an existing activity and making it better?

Nothing is too small or trivial at this stage: I've met students who say, 'But I haven't really done anything. I've not been in a sports team, or helped in a student society.' There's usually something, however – I have yet to meet anyone who does academic work, and *nothing* else. It might be serious computer gaming, organising a journal club once or twice in the academic subject, being active on social media, having great online research skills, getting people together for a party – any of these can start to give you clues as to what you like doing and what is important to you.

Get a pen and a sheet of paper and finish the following sentence: 'The following are really important to me and I get a lot of satisfaction from . . .'

When you've done that, we can go on to the second stage, closely connected with the 'What do you want?' question.

## WHAT ARE YOU GOOD AT?

It is likely that the things you've been doing over the years, outside school/college/work (and indeed inside as well), are activities that you're quite good at. If we enjoy things, we do more of them, we get better at them, and we enjoy them more. It may not feel that way when you're practising the piano, learning vocabulary, rehearsing music or a play, painting or drawing another sketch, or practising football skills on a wet Wednesday afternoon, but if you've kept going (sometimes with the 'encouragement' of teachers and parents), you have got better, and enjoyed them more.

Your next list (get a pencil and paper and let's do this in the next five minutes) is to finish the following sentence: 'I'm really good at . . .'

Be as specific or abstract as you like. Some abstract ideas: persuading others, inspiring others, empathising with people, working well in a team, leading, communicating, presenting, writing, networking, explaining things, and creating new ideas. Some more specific ideas: computer programming, architectural design, carpentry, cooking, medical diagnosis, chemical analysis, solving maths problems, and so on.

You'll have noticed that I'm not giving a list of a hundred keywords for you to pick and choose from – it's important for you to come up with your own list. It may not be complete in the next five minutes but make a start and other words will come to you over the next few days – add them to your list.

Sometimes you'll hear about 'soft' skills and 'hard' skills. I think these are somewhat pejorative terms, as they seem to value the so-called soft skills below those of hard skills. But the soft skills, like the abstract ones listed above, are what make the world go round. The hard skills, like the specific ones listed above, are perhaps easier to measure. Employers want them both, perhaps to different degrees depending on what level you are at in the organisation.

## MIND THE GAP

Look at your lists (the one you've written about what is important to you and the one about what you are good at). Any obvious gaps? Now might be a good time to think about what someone who is going to pay you will be looking for – then, if there are any obvious gaps, you could think about doing something new, or developing something you already do, to fill the gap.

Everyone has their own list of what are employability skills – what skills you should have to persuade someone that you'd be ideal to be working for them. I tend to use a version of the eight skills that the Confederation of British Industry (CBI) defined in their Future Fit report from 2008, listed in the table below.

When you look at the list, think about what examples you have for each one – to make it easier, score it with one of three marks: 0 (for none), ~ (for some), and ✔ (for OK for now). As you fill in your examples, make sure you think widely about all your activities, including in academic work, social life, formal and informal extracurricular activities.

## EIGHT EMPLOYABILITY SKILLS

| Skill | Examples | Your example | Your score |
|---|---|---|---|
| Communications | Inter/intrapersonal skills, listening, observing, speaking, questioning, analysing, and evaluating | | |
| Leadership | Ability to motivate, influence and lead others | | |
| Team working | Respecting others, co-operating, negotiating/persuading, contributing to discussions, awareness of the interdependence of others | | |
| Planning & Organising | Scheduling resources, time management, multi-tasking and meeting objectives | | |
| Initiative & Problem solving | Analysing facts and situations, applying creative thinking to develop appropriate solutions | | |
| Self management | Readiness to accept responsibility, flexibility, resilience, self-starting, appropriate assertiveness, | | |

| | |
|---|---|
| | time management, readiness to improve own performance based on feedback and reflective learning |
| Business & Customer awareness | Basic understanding of the key drivers for business success – including the importance of innovation and taking calculated risks – and the need to provide customer satisfaction and build customer loyalty |
| Entrepreneurship & Enterprise | An ability to demonstrate an innovative approach, creativity, collaboration and risk taking |

There will be some other skills for your list, that are technical – these might be languages, (computer) coding, statistical analysis, spreadsheets, and so on.

Look at the list, your examples and how you have scored. Highlight the skills that score '0' – these are your high priority; the others with a ~ are your lower priority. What can you do to gain or improve those skills that scored 0 and to have some examples you can talk about? In your course, at work, in your social life?

## THE MAP EMERGES FROM THE FOG

The two lists, what you value and what you are good at, start to run together. Career nirvana is probably 'doing what you want to do, and doing it well': you'll know because people will tell you you're good or you can measure that it's good. However, the two lists are not static; they will change over time. You'll learn on the job, see opportunities, meet others and fall in love, and the world outside also changes: technology brings new organisations and ways of working, and new challenges emerge, such as climate change, resource limitation, migration, and the economy, to name just a few.

## Balancing the role

Most of us want to do more of what we are good at, and less of what we don't really enjoy. Note the word 'less', not 'none'. Every job has parts we wouldn't choose to do, but are essential. For you, it might be revising documents, presenting reports, cold calling customers, or travelling abroad every week. If you can see that it is essential for your role, is of a manageable amount, and can explain to yourself (and maybe others) why you do it, then it'll probably be OK and you'll be able to live with it.

When the undesirable parts get too much, your circumstances change, or your values alter, then it's time to dust off this book and start thinking – can you change the role, to reduce the bad parts back to a manageable level (for example, the amount of travel) or is it time to find a new role?

## What's on the map?

You know roughly what you are looking for in a role, the sort of organisation and what you are good at. Armed with this vital understanding and definition of what you want and can do, now's the time to research what is out there. Students tend to know about quite a limited set of jobs – teaching and lecturing, what they've seen on TV or the cinema, what their parents and friends' parents do. But there are more jobs than detectives, chefs, forensic scientists, footballers and pop singers – and new jobs are coming along all the time.

I recently met a student studying maths who was reluctantly applying to be an actuary – he enjoyed maths and wanted to use it in his job. He had selected actuarial work because someone in his immediate family was in the same business. He said he was not aware of any other jobs where he could use his maths. I suggested a few to open the conversation.

'Oh, my dream is to teach, but my family say I'll be no good, though I think I would be,' he said.

It was time for him to start some research, beyond the boundaries set or implied by his family.

## Exploring the map

It's all around you, the information you need. Careers Services at school, college, and university are awash with guides about industries and organisations that operate in those industries. Even once you've left, you can usually go back and collect guides – and if you've moved away, then call or drop by your local college or university. Then there are third-party organisations like councils that put on careers events.

A careers fair is a highly efficient way to meet dozens of people who work in different organisations, in a really short time – if you do go to a careers fair, make sure you're well prepared with questions, that you have a notebook to record information you learn, that you know which organisations will be there and who specifically you might want to meet. Dress quite well and be ready to explain in two sentences the sort of thing you are looking for.

Then, of course, there's online research. You can start with university careers websites that are open access, and there are also any number of other sites, such as Prospects and Target, that can help. These will give you general advice; for specific information about one organisation, head for its own website. There should be a section on 'Careers' or 'Employment opportunities'.

As you start to focus on one particular track or direction on your own career map, you may well find it useful to start talking to people who work at the organisation or in the same industry. Information Interviewing is a very powerful way for you to gain valuable knowledge; you can read much more about Information Interviewing in another section.

## WHAT DO YOU DO ON MONDAY MORNING?

All the best plans and ideas in the world are useless until you take action. Anyone can have ideas, but very, very few people do something about them – so if you do take action, you will stand out.

If you are prevaricating, at least recognise that you are doing so consciously. There's always Facebook to check, friends to call up, that book to read, that film to watch, that sports game to go to, driving lesson, rehearsal, trip to London for the weekend, clothes to wash, room to tidy, pencils to sharpen and on, and on. (Recognise any of these?)

There are endless apps and suggestions for how to make lists, fix priorities, set your own targets. In the end, you know what works for you – keep it simple and focus on the outcome, not the process. Start with a pen and paper, or a simple To Do list. Don't waste money and, more importantly, don't get distracted by processes that promise to increase your efficiency.

I would suggest some behaviour that reinforces success – that's why you may have had a sticker chart on the fridge at home to mark when you'd brushed your teeth or tidied your room. Small achievements, obvious rewards, always visible. So, set yourself some small targets that are reasonably achievable: get CV drafted by Friday, make two phone calls for an Information Interview in the next week, research three law firms by next Wednesday, email two contacts tonight. Getting used to saying 'Done' makes you feel good.

To quote from Nike, 'Just do it.'

## THE CV: A MEANS TO MANY ENDS

The first action that tells you you're getting serious about starting a job search is probably when you sit down to write a CV.

There are plenty of templates, examples and even whole books on CVs – as well as people and organisations offering to write your CV for you, for a handsome fee. By all means, consider using these services, but I believe that if you read the next few pages you will be quite capable of writing a pretty decent first draft, showing it to one or two people, then polishing it up and using it effectively.

## What's a CV for?

An aside: CV stands for *Curriculum Vitae*, a Latin phrase that can be roughly translated as 'the course of my life'. A similar document is known, particularly in the US, as a *Résumé*, from the French for 'summary'. Perhaps we have come to use foreign terms for this document to give it an air of mystery and make it sound more difficult to produce than it really is.

First, what's the point of a CV? Not such a flippant question, because if you know why you're doing something, you're usually more motivated to do it and you'll get a better result. Number one: a CV is only to get you the interview or the meeting; it is not aimed at getting you the job. I think it's safe to assume that no one has been hired solely on his or her CV. It should contain just enough to intrigue the reader with your background, skills and experiences but not so much that it either bores the reader or gives them some random reason to reject your application.

### Give them the evidence

Evidence makes all the difference, and lack of evidence is just assertion. I'd advise you not to write the sentences you sometimes see at the top of CVs that assert:

'A strong team player with superb analytical skills, also happy to work alone. Very high attention to detail, yet able to see the big picture. Finely honed presentation and writing skills and able to communicate well with small or large groups.'

Anyone can write these lines, but without evidence they are very weak. Don't do it.

Thinking again about the reader, let's make it easy for them by presenting the CV in a format that they're expecting, including a simple overall structure. I would work with three sections: Education, Experience, and Skills/Community Activities/ Interests (you can choose the exact title headings you prefer). For the first few years after graduating from university or college, you'll put Education first, and then one day it will move to be the last section.

**Education**: List your most recent and relevant courses. For a student it's probably your degree and A-levels or IB or BTEC. Give the subject and result. No need to go back to the result of your spelling test in Year 4. By your mid-20s, you can drop the school exams. List any prizes and awards here. Don't give intense detail around your final-year dissertation subject. If any one subject or project stands out, then list it with the result you achieved.

**Experience**: Separate headings, with some detail in two or three bullets, listed in reverse chronological order (latest first) of your experiences. I'd put everything under this heading, whether paid or unpaid, student activities and societies, or summer work experience or internship – to me, it's all experience.

**Interests**: This section is to show how you do more than work, that you can chat about things outside work. It doesn't matter what the subject is, but you must give some detail so that the reader can start a conversation. In some interviews, the recruiter will start in this section with the aim of relaxing you.

Bad example: 'Travel, hockey, cooking, reading, socialising with friends, cinema, music.'

Everyone does these things, to a greater or lesser extent, and it gives the reader nothing really extra about you.

Better version: 'Travel to European capitals to visit cathedrals – six so far. Play hockey for school/college 2nd XI: weekly matches and training sessions. Cooking, recently learning to cook Asian cuisine. Cinema, particularly French films from the last thirty years. Play in a rock band, mostly for our own pleasure, but have survived two open mic nights.'

(You don't need and won't have all of these – two to three will be fine.)

With each section, focus on demonstrating your responsibilities, achievements and how you're a good colleague or team player. It can help you to draft how you describe each role you had by finishing the following two sentences:

★ 'I am/was responsible for . . .'
★ 'My achievements include/d . . .'

Most student CVs I read are peppered with dull <u>process</u> words:

★ '<u>Worked</u> in the Finance Office on a project to write new reports on customer accounts.'
★ '<u>Organised</u> speaker events for the international student society.'
★ '<u>Lifeguarding</u> at local swimming pool.'

The problem with this is the reader has no concept of what work you did, how long for (an afternoon? three months?), who you reported to, whether the work achieved anything, and how much of the work you were responsible for (rather than what the other members of the team did).

So we could rewrite the above examples:

★ 'Responsible to the Finance Office Section Leader for creating and implementing new, weekly reports on defaulting customer accounts, now used throughout the office.'
★ 'Elected as Events Organiser for international student society, responsible for arranging weekly lectures throughout term.'
★ 'Appointed lifeguard for local swimming pool; solely responsible for all safety aspects of pool and users, both in and out of the water, during regular afternoon shifts.'

If you remember the earlier point, that a CV should bring in evidence of your achievements (not just assertion), then you can see that adding in 'elected' or 'appointed' brings in that vital third-party evidence. In the same way, your GCSEs, A-levels, IB, BTEC, degree and so on provide third-party evidence that you have reached certain academic standards.

Next, bring the descriptions of your responsibilities and achievements alive with numbers and detail. Don't give away commercial secrets, use ranges if you can't remember or never collected the exact results, but if you include some hard data it makes your descriptions so much more interesting, and shows the reader that you understand the importance of measuring activity.

So a further rewrite:

★ 'Responsible to the Finance Office Section Leader for creating and implementing new, weekly reports on 100–200 defaulting customer accounts, now used throughout the four finance departments.'

★ 'Elected as Events Organiser for international student society, responsible for arranging ten weekly lectures throughout term. Grew average weekly attendance at the lectures from twelve to twenty-five students.'

★ 'Appointed lifeguard for local swimming pool that hosted twenty to two hundred swimmers each session; solely responsible for all safety aspects of pool and users, both in and out of the water, during regular four-hour shifts.'

While it's relatively clear how to describe your responsibilities and achievements, it might be more difficult to show why you'd be a great colleague to have around. This is where you need to be able to talk about teams you have been involved in – not necessarily led or been elected to senior roles – for example, playing on a sports team, working in a shop, helping to stage a drama production or being a member of a choir or orchestra, all demonstrate that you work well with others, and that you turn up come rain or shine (particularly for outdoor sports . . .).

## Form AND content

Layout is important as first impressions count: is this a simple to read, well-presented document? Test yourself: if you were receiving this, would you find it attractive and welcoming, or frankly a bit of a struggle? Don't expect your reader to work too hard to dig out the important parts of your CV – if they have a hundred or more to read, they just may not do it justice.

Some top tips for layout: keep it short, no more than two pages for a business CV, but you can have more for an academic CV. A readable and clear font – 10-point is the absolute minimum, though you might use 11- or 12-point for the headings. Leave some blank space around and within the document – give it some 'air', so don't squeeze the text all the way up to the edge of the paper – not only does it looked jammed, it also might not all print out.

Use bullet points for the details and, given you'll be short of space, condense the language. This isn't the time for flowing poetic English, but crisp, focused points.

---

**Blowing your own trumpet or gauche exaggeration?**

There's a balance to be had – and you have to decide what you are comfortable with – in how much you sell yourself and how you describe your achievements. This is not the time for muted understatement: if you've played at Wimbledon, you should say more than 'I play tennis from time to time.' On the other hand, if you spent two days work shadowing a local barrister, then it would be unwise to write, 'I represented a client in a high-profile trial.'

Stick to the facts (third-party evidence is powerful) but make sure you include all the key facts. For example, if you were *elected* by the student body (however few actually voted), then include that – it's a strong endorsement by others; if you had the idea and collected a team around you for Young Enterprise, then tell them – not just 'worked in a team'.

---

## Passing the two-second test

Once you've created a first draft, print it out. Try folding it vertically and skim reading just the left-hand half – are all the key words and messages there? Your reader will initially spend just *two or three seconds* glancing at your beautifully crafted CV: research shows that people skim a whole page following a capital letter F – down the left, across the top and maybe across the middle. So key responsibility and achievement words have to be at the start of each line, on the left-hand side.

You can find lists of these power words in many job brochures and websites – but since this is meant to be a personal CV, I'd rather you made this personal and didn't copy lists and templates from somewhere. Otherwise, your CV will look like everyone else's. So, no lists of words here. But when you read down the left-hand side, do you see your qualifications? Any awards? Name of the organisation where you worked or had work experience or volunteered? Bullet points that start: Implemented . . . Responsible for . . . Designed . . . Produced . . .?

> **Should I include this?**
>
> The other day, I'd spent fifteen minutes discussing a CV with a student and he seemed happy with the ideas we'd covered. As he got to the door, ready to leave, he turned and asked, 'Should I put my five languages on my CV as well?'
>
> What may be commonplace to you might be outstanding to someone else.

Is there anything on your CV that is not relevant? Do they really need at this stage to know your date of birth? More than one address? Your clean driving licence? Marital status? Referees? Almost certainly not. In fact some of these could lead to discrimination (age, marital status, sexual orientation to name three).

Other areas of potential discrimination are, of course, gender, race and disability. Depending on your name, your CV is going to be more or less explicit about your gender and/or race. It would be naïve to suggest that there isn't discrimination on these grounds – and indeed there is plenty of evidence that when presented with two identical CVs, apart from one bearing a man's name and one a woman's, some recruiters give the man's more weight. For the avoidance of doubt, some students put their citizenship on a CV (thus pre-empting the Right to Work or Visa question). But the gender, race and disability question is not all or nothing: employers are increasingly aware and wanting to recruit from the widest possible pool of applicants, some are running programmes to attract women, black and minority ethnic applicants, and disabled applicants, and promote their membership of, for example, Stonewall, to demonstrate that they are Lesbian, Gay, Bisexual, Transgender, Questioning (LGBTQ)-friendly.

Since we can't second-guess the recruiter, and you want to show how open and honest you are, I think the best you can do is go forward with your CV and application – aware of the potential issues (I'll talk about coping with discrimination in Part Three) but not being driven by them.

Final step: polish to perfection. I've seen too many CVs from applicants and students that claim the writer has 'great attention to detail' and then has a typo or poor punctuation. Remember we don't want to give the reader the slightest reason to reject you before they've met you – so make sure the font is all the same and consistent, the words are all spelled correctly (don't rely on a spell checker), the words are all the ones you meant (for example, 'from' instead of 'form') the grammar is correct, and the tone is consistent. Check that the verbs are all in the same form; maybe all in the present (for current role) and past tenses or maybe participle form (that is, the same '-ing' form throughout).

Simple check: print it out and read it out loud. Somehow the audible mouth-to-ear route to your brain will help you pick up sentences that sound odd or ambiguous. We'll mention this again about cover letters.

Now you can go public – show it to someone else. If you're a non-native English speaker, and it's an English CV, then show it to a friend who is a native speaker and ask them to read it. They'll pick up subtleties and nuances that you may have missed. If it's a CV for a region you're unfamiliar with, ask a local what they expect: for example, photographs are expected on French CVs.

(Don't put them on British CVs.) Listen carefully to feedback and edit the CV if necessary.

Last point: there's no such thing as one CV – you'll want to adapt it slightly for each audience. You may want to emphasise certain roles, or responsibilities, depending on who is going to be reading it.

## COVER LETTERS AND APPLICATION FORMS

Most job applications will ask for a statement on how you fit the selection criteria, as well as a CV. This might take the form of a 'cover letter' to go with your CV, or might be a series of questions on an application form (on paper or, more commonly now, on a website) that effectively ask the questions that you should be answering unprompted in a letter. You may also use a cover letter when requesting an Information Interview to introduce yourself and justify why the recipient should spare you some time.

Some recruiters read the letter first and ignore the CV, or scan the CV quickly and then focus on the letter; either way, your letter deserves some thought.

For most of us, including students, letter writing is less commonplace – the days of writing to granny to thank her for the birthday present are receding. This means we are out of practice in how to write a letter. Most students' first draft cover letters I see betray this: they tend to be stiff and formal to begin with and only start to come alive in the third paragraph. Starting at the third paragraph may not be such a bad idea – even if logically impossible – but perhaps having written a flowing third paragraph you could revisit the other paragraphs and rewrite them?

As with a CV, you are using the cover letter to inspire the reader to want to meet you – to hook them in at the beginning, convince them that you are attracted to their organisation, intrigue them with some inspiring details of what you have done, and state what you would like to happen next. If you were receiving such a letter, think about what you would like to read, and what would make you want to help.

Some tips for a cover letter: keep it to one page (of A4), use four main paragraphs (I'll describe each of these below), and above all, make it personal. Use direct language and be specific where you can. Try to avoid 'management-speak' and jargon that can end up sounding too general and, therefore, very uninteresting and strangely disconnected from the real world.

An ideal style lies somewhere between texting and historical letters from the last century; between 'hey, it wld be cool to meet' and 'I respectfully ask you to consider my request to engage in a short meeting wherein we could talk about the activities of your establishment.' Professional and friendly – remember you want them to want to meet (and maybe work with) you.

Needless to say, though perhaps not so needless, each letter should be tailored for the organisation. If you are making several applications to organisations in a similar industry, then be really careful if you cut and paste. I've seen too many letters that start:

'Dear Accenture, I've always wanted to work at EY . . .'

. . . and you can imagine what happens to that letter.

Turning to application forms: aside from the usual name, subject, education details, an application form will often have three or four questions for you to answer in, for example, 250 words or fewer. Questions will be similar to those you can expect at interview, for example:

★ Describe a time when you led a project.
★ What two aspects of consumer marketing are going to change in the next five years?
★ What attracts you to Widget International?

★ Give three examples that show how you are well suited to a role in finance.

Draft them separately, check the word count, read them out loud, and then cut and paste into the application form.

## Four sections in a classic cover letter

Like a good conversation or introduction during an Information Interview, a cover letter sets out to tell the reader why they should listen and what you would like them to do next. There's a top, two core sections, and a tail:

1. Open (top): explain why the reader should keep reading – 'hook' them in.
2. Them: what it is about them or their organisation that has prompted you to write the letter.
3. You: a highlight or two about you that intrigues them and demonstrates your credentials.
4. Close (tail): a warm close and a call to action – what happens next.

## 1. OPEN

Who you are, what you are studying, where you are now working, or where you are about to start studying. No need to put your name here, it's at the bottom of the letter and on the attached CV. Include any personal connection: 'Javed Duval kindly suggested I get in touch to . . .' State what you are asking for:

'I am pleased to be applying for the role of . . .' or

'I am writing to ask if you would consider meeting me for a short Information Interview'.

About two to four sentences, or three to four lines.

## 2. THEM

Your chance to demonstrate what you know about the organisation and why you have singled them out for this letter and your request. Avoid quoting their corporate mission statement or other marketing materials from their website – it's lazy and they know what's on their website already. To keep the reader interested, you'll want to show how you have done some work to come to your conclusion that you want to meet them or apply for a job. You might have talked to some current employees or read some background materials – you could quote this and add some of your own assessment, for example in relation to what other organisations have been doing.

One excellent reason to attend careers fairs, talk to alumni of your school or college, or read the press (in print or online) is that you can gather useful information about organisations – not just to weave into letters like this, but because it will inform your decision-making about whether you want to write or apply in the first place.

I'm reluctant to give examples, since your letter must be in your own style, but you might be able to start this paragraph with something like:

'I was inspired to learn from Mary Jones, when I met her at the recent company presentation on campus, that Widget International really does take customer service and staff development seriously. She confirmed what I had read in the *Financial Times* (08/07/15), that Widget International spends 2 per cent of revenues on training – higher than any other firm in the sector.'

About a hundred words, or five or six sentences, or six or seven lines.

## 3. YOU

The longest section of the letter, in which you intrigue the reader so they'd like to take the next step (which you helpfully tell them in the fourth paragraph). Try not to repeat details from your CV, since you may well be attaching this to the letter. This section is your chance to go into more detail around one or two of the activities on the CV, explaining your motivation, activities and results. You'll pick some examples that are relevant to the opportunity for which you are applying, or, if you are asking for an information meeting, that are relevant to the reader.

Be as specific as you can, without giving away trade secrets, as detail can bring the activity alive for the reader; they can relate to the challenge you faced and effectively share it with you. Just as with your CV, include some numeric data where relevant to demonstrate that you are numerate, recognise the importance of measuring things, and to bring the activity further alive for the reader. An example:

'When I was on the committee for the student drama society, I was responsible for marketing the termly shows, trying to fill a theatre with three hundred seats for four nights. I quickly learned to use a variety of promotional techniques, including putting up posters in twenty high-traffic areas around campus, running unique Facebook campaigns, actively tweeting the event, asking for links to other student society websites, and adding the event to all the cast and crew's email signatures. We almost filled the house each night and asked people who came how they had heard about the event; 75 per cent said it was from Facebook so we used that channel more often in subsequent shows.'

Up to about 150 words, or nine or ten sentences, or ten to twelve lines.

## 4. CLOSE

In the last two or three lines, you can confirm how you feel about what you are asking for and say what you'd like to happen – what marketing people describe as a 'call to action'. If it's a job application, you can demonstrate that you recognise there is a formal process ahead. For example: 'I am excited to be applying for the role of X at Widget International' or, if you're asking for a meeting: 'I look forward to meeting you and will give you a call in a couple of days to see when might be mutually possible.'

Try not to include any threats or put any actions on them that are, by definition, out of your control, for example, 'I look forward to explaining more at interview'. I've also read applications that state: 'I hope you will take my application seriously'. Not good.

Nor would I waste space with 'Please do not hesitate to get in touch if you need any further information' since they will do that anyway, or will wait until they meet you at interview.

If you want to close professionally, you could write something like:

'I look forward to hearing from you once you have had a chance to review my application.'

Finally, if you are going to use 'Yours sincerely' or 'Yours faithfully', remember that the first one is used if you are writing to a named person, the second if you have written 'Dear Sir/Madam'. It may be a small detail, but applications have been rejected when the wrong one was used.

> **Follow through . . .**
> If you write that you'll phone to follow up, then make sure you do. Mark your diary, put a note somewhere you'll see it, and phone. If you don't get through the first time, try again.

### . . . and confirm

When an employer writes you an email to confirm when you are coming, whether it's a job or a week's work experience, reply to confirm you received the note, that you're still coming, and you're looking forward to it. It's professional and means they're not left guessing.

I've met students who had not replied to emails from schools confirming their work shadowing – and the schools contacted us to see if the students were still coming.

And when you receive a job offer, reply to thank them, even if you want to wait a day or two to consider it.

## The exception – answering the listed criteria

There is an exception to the one-page limit for a cover letter: where you have to show how you meet some defined selection criteria. Some job ads will say: 'Please show how you meet each of the selection criteria' – and somewhere else in the ad it will list out the **essential** and **desirable** criteria. Such a recruiter is making it really easy for you, and if you ignore their request, you are making it really difficult for them.

If they have five applicants, they'll probably do the extra work and decode your letter against their criteria; however, if they have fifty applications, I'm not so sure they'll spend the time. I'm certain that at school your teachers told you that the best tip for exams was RTQ-ATQ: Read The Question and Answer The Question. Good advice then and here as well.

So, if a recruiter has gone to the trouble of asking you to show how you meet each of the criteria that they have helpfully listed – then do just that. One by one. Your letter might become two or even three pages – but that's OK. You should know that the recruiter has a checklist of each criterion and will be marking each one as they read your application.

As an applicant, you want the employer to put a series of ticks and no '?s' or 'Don't knows' on the checklist when assessing your application. If your letter is already well structured and the reader can see that you've gone through each point, you'll be ahead *before* the reader even starts reading – and may well give you the benefit of the doubt on some points.

If you find you actually don't meet one or two of their 'essential' criteria, then you've an uphill struggle ahead – this may be a good chance to not waste time and move on, once you have double-checked that you don't meet the criteria. Look out for criteria that end 'or equivalent'. You may not have that essential Masters degree, but you have other qualifications or experience you can explain as equivalent.

On the other hand, no applicant will meet all the criteria perfectly so don't be put off if you think you are a 75 per cent fit. You'll need to explain how your *other* experience or skills effectively help you meet all the criteria.

It is often repeated that women look at a job description and say, 'I can only meet 80 per cent of the criteria, I'd better not apply,' whereas men look at the same description and say, 'I meet 30 per cent of the criteria, I'll be perfect.' The men reading this need no further encouragement, the women need to feel they can apply, even with 'only' an 80 per cent fit.

## GRAMMAR – PEDANTRY OR BEAUTY?

Language is about communication – so as long as you get your message over, that's all that matters, right? Well, no. It's also about showing that you are professional, know the rules and can follow the rules. The reader is also subconsciously checking that, if you were working for that organisation, you would be a good ambassador when it came to communicating with clients and colleagues.

Some basics – and I admit some of these are my own sensitivities:

★ Use short sentences, with simple subordinate clauses. Ideally, put the point of the sentence first, rather than some long lead-in clause.
★ Use Anglo-Saxon rooted words rather than their Latin/French equivalent. 'Find out' rather than 'ascertain'; 'near' rather than 'adjacent'; 'new' rather than 'novel'.
★ Use the apostrophe correctly, especially with 'its' and 'it's' and plural possessives (for example, student's and students'). If it is just a plural of an abbreviation, then no need for an apostrophe (that is, 'CDs' not 'CD's').
★ If in doubt, use a dictionary to check differences in homonyms such as between 'principle' and 'principal'; 'accept' and 'except'; and 'practice' and 'practise'.
★ Check every phrase, especially for colloquialisms. For example, you rarely need the phrase 'in order to' when 'to' will do just fine; you don't need to 'meet with', just 'meet'; you don't get 'off of' anything, just 'off'; 'many' is always better than 'lots of'; do not use shortenings such as 'we'll' or 'I've' – it's 'we will' and 'I have'.
★ Avoid the very overused words in CVs and cover letters: these include 'honed' (if it's about your skills, try 'developed'); 'passion' (try 'enthusiasm', 'energy', 'interest').
★ As for CVs, if you're a non-native English speaker, then try to find someone who is a native English speaker to read it over.

Finally, print it out, stand up and, with a pencil in hand, read it aloud. You'll be surprised at what you notice that looked great on the screen but now sounds clumsy, is unclear, is too long a sentence, is a non sequitur, or is ambiguous. Give yourself enough time that you can sleep on it and read it one last time in the morning; remember, unless there was a midnight deadline, the recipient is unlikely to be reading their office emails at midnight, so get up early, read your precious and important cover letter one last time, edit if necessary, and send it in first thing.

In the days before email and computers, people dictated letters, someone typed them and one or two days later they came back for signature. I suspect (and from my own experience, ahem) many mistakes were avoided when dictated letters were reread later: 'Did I really write that? Well, thank goodness I hadn't sent it yet.' This was a successful way to catch egregious errors. While it's very difficult to be a writer and an editor at the same time, try to build in some delay or change of pace to your creative process to give yourself a chance to review things.

### Email, phone or letter?

Which form of communication is best? Which should you use? One rule of thumb is use the one they have used to you – if they email you, email back. If you are starting the communication, use one then follow up with another.

If you want to be distinctive, use an unusual method or style – very few business letters are sent these days, so an elegant, hand-written letter can stand out in certain situations (though probably odd if going for a job in IT).

## EMAIL ETIQUETTE

The way you use email can say a lot about you, so it needs a little care. If in doubt about what you've written, try to delay pressing the Send button. We can add 'the sent email' to the Arabian proverb that says: 'Four things come not back: the spoken word, the sped arrow, the past life and the neglected opportunity.'

Emails are strong for facts and weak for emotion or persuasion. They are perfect for confirming information: here's the address, this is when we'll meet, and here are the data we discussed. They are a very poor way to either show emotion or to persuade someone to do something. Emails can be easily misinterpreted because they are usually so short – and are often skim-read so the reader might miss the point.

Effective communication is mostly made by body language, somewhat by how you say things, and only a little by what you actually say. So email has reduced the communication to the smallest part of this: only the words with no tone of voice – small wonder it can be misinterpreted.

Emails do become more effective if you have met each other, or work together, as the reader can hear your voice when they read – but to begin with it's not the best method of persuasion. Which is why the phone can be much more effective in persuading someone to have that Information Interview with you. And phone calls can't be deleted as easily as emails, where one click can delete your message – and you'll never know why.

Employers told me at a recent meeting that students can either be too brief, with little introductory warmth or charm, or too long with too much detail. Write as though talking to a teacher or tutor that you don't know very well. Use a formal title for the first message and then change to first names or other, if they invite you to do so in their response. As in all communication, try to put yourself in the reader's shoes – how would *you* feel if you received this note? Would *you* want to help?

## THE TELEPHONE
We don't use the phone as much as we used to because we now have texting, Facebook messaging, email, Instagram, WhatsApp,

Snapchat, Twitter, and many other ways to communicate without speaking. So, we're out of practice and perhaps worried about how to make calls, particularly to strangers. On the other hand, if you do make a call, you'll stand out and you'll also find that you gain more from the conversation than if you'd just messaged someone.

How often have you texted back and forth, perhaps ten or twenty times, with a friend to agree when and where to meet? Assuming you were both able to speak out loud (not in a lecture/at the cinema), wouldn't a two-minute call have been quicker and, actually, more fun?

If you need any further persuasion that the phone can be a good way to communicate, then think about this: speaking to people is much more interesting and rewarding – you may learn extra information, you can persuade and charm people, arrange meetings quickly, or generate an emotional bond. You can also instantly clarify what you said, if it was unclear or the other person misunderstood.

On the phone, you can also find out why they don't want or can't do what you're asking – really valuable information that you would be unlikely to learn by text or email. And having learned what their objection is, you can perhaps find an alternative. In another section, I talk about how when people say 'No' it rarely means never; it might mean 'not now' or 'not that long'. If you explore this on the phone, you might be able to find an alternative time, or to clarify that you don't need that amount of time.

Phoning up for feedback after an interview can give you much more useful information than an email request – you might be able to elicit more details on what went well and where you could improve for the next round or next time.

## TIPS FOR PHONE CALLS

If it helps, jot down the main points you want to make, or the questions you want to ask. To begin with you might find a script helpful – though you don't want to sound like someone coldcalling about double-glazing.

For an important call, it can be energising to stand up. Obviously find somewhere quiet, with no distractions – driving, walking, reading email, listening to music, and watching TV are probably going to be distracting and will limit your engagement. If you're on a crowded train, then you'll probably feel inhibited by others listening in.

If the interviewer or recruiter phones you, and you are not somewhere quiet or able to take the call immediately, you should feel able to ask the caller to wait a few moments while you move somewhere you won't be disturbed.

For a really important call like an interview, make sure you dress as though you were meeting face-to-face. Like all dressing, a big benefit is to get you in the best frame of mind.

If you do have a script or some notes and headings of what you'd like to cover, then make sure that you still listen to what is being said; don't be afraid to ask for clarification, say if you don't know something, and stop when you've finished your answer. There's more advice on interviewing in a later section, all of which can apply here.

## INFORMATION INTERVIEWING

'Networking' – perhaps the most overused word in job searching and the one that most of us run away from. The very word can conjure up scenes of mingling with distinguished and senior people, and being sparkling and brilliant in just twenty seconds. As it happens, meeting other people, who may be able to help you with advice (and just maybe a job), can be really helpful – as well as frightening. So if the pressure to shine can make the best of us tongue-tied, is there a better way?

Instead of 'networking', think of this activity as Information Interviewing – you're having a chat with someone to offer and gain information. You might do this in a crowded room, in the corridor, or in a short meeting in their office or a café. If your aim is to gain only some information (and not a job), then you're likely to be successful, and start to build a relationship and some insight into possible careers or industry sectors.

### What is an Information Interview?

The ideal is a ten- to fifteen-minute one-to-one meeting with someone who can give you information about an industry, a job, an organisation or a career that you are interested in. You are there to learn – as a result of such a meeting you may decide not to think about that industry any more, or you may get quite excited about what you're learning. During the meeting, you can ask about a typical day at work, the challenges facing the industry, what qualifications you might need, what sort of background people have who work there, why they like their job and industry and so on. With active listening (see more details below in 'Face-to-Face meetings'), you'll have more than enough to fill ten to fifteen minutes – and usually people will give you more time.

### Information Interviewing: at least six benefits

First, it's not a job interview so there's much less pressure on you and on them – you will be more **relaxed**. Do not do a 'hard sell' – you're not trying to sell yourself. Indeed, there's a world of difference between ringing someone and asking for a job and asking for an Information Interview. If they don't have any jobs right there and then (what are the odds?), then it's a very short conversation; however, if you ask for an Information Interview, they'll probably be intrigued, ask you what one of those is, and then agree to spend ten minutes with you.

Second, you will learn about an industry or company; after you've done a few of these, you'll be able to give some information back and feed in what you've learned from other meetings: 'When I met X from ABC, she described the challenges facing this sector as including 1, 2 and 3 – is that your view?'

Third, you get to polish the way you present yourself, the questions you ask, the way you describe your background and what you are looking for; remember, it's not a job interview so if you say something not quite right, you can polish it up for next time.

The fourth benefit is that you get to stay in control of your whole job search process, showing the people you are meeting that you're the sort of person who takes control of their career. One alternative will have been to send off hundreds of applications and then sit back and wait for *someone else* to decide about you; you'll probably have to do some of this, but with Information Interviewing, you'll feel in more control.

Fifth, if you make a good impression, then it can happen that a few weeks or months later, your contact will call you to see if you are interested in a project or job they now have available. You were someone who showed initiative, who was interested in the sector, who seems to be someone who takes control and would be good to have around – rather than going through advertising a job (though of course many organisations have to do this), they will see if you are available, especially if it's just a short project. This is the so-called 'hidden' job market. Even if there is a formal application process, they may well draw your attention to the job so you can apply.

Sixth, you start to build your network of people that you have met and who have been helpful.

At this stage, you may ask why anyone would do this for you. The fact is that some won't, but most will – in the same way that you would help if someone asked you, for example, about your school, college, university, hobby, job, A-levels, apprenticeship, or degree course.

I met a graduate student recently who had been having some Information Interviews, and seemed to know the basics.

'Thing is,' he said, 'it's not working. I've had a few meetings with people in the insurance industry and I've now decided it's just not for me.'

This, though, was still a pretty good outcome for him; he had used this approach to eliminate an industry sector from his job search. Much better than applying for jobs and maybe getting one – only to find out months or years later that it wasn't what he wanted to do.

### Model Information Interviewing: how to do it, step by step

You've decided which industry sectors you are interested in, and have just met a really interesting person, or heard someone inspiring speak at your school or college: now's the time to get in touch to ask if they would spare ten to fifteen minutes of their time for an Information Interview. If you don't have any contacts immediately, then think of the people you do know and who they might know. At this stage you can be really creative – your parents' friends, your friends' parents, teachers, tutors, supervisors, social groups, and alumni of your school, college or university.

Now comes the scary part: you have to contact them, but it's easier than you think because you will have some sort of connection via your friends, tutors, etc., etc. It's important that it's you who contacts them – not someone on your behalf. Email and then ideally follow up with a phone call. Find out their correct title, and spelling of their name if it's not obvious, before you write your note – you can do this by checking LinkedIn or phoning the organisation and speaking to the receptionist or to their secretary. 'I want to write to Mrs X and wanted to check their title and how they spell their name.' In your introductory email you might write something like:

Dear Mr/Mrs/Ms/Dr/Professor X,

I am a Xth-year student at XYZ, studying for a degree / A-levels in X and exploring my options for what to do when I leave. I am very interested in the X industry and have already worked on projects on X/been involved in the X student society.

I wonder if you would be willing to spare ten minutes of your time for an Information Interview? Naturally, I would be able to come to your office to meet.

I will give you a call in a couple of days to see if we can find a mutually agreeable time.

With best wishes,

Your name

So that last part, confirming that you will call to follow up, is going to be more frightening but can be the difference between getting a meeting or not. So do try to do it.

Then, with a meeting set up, it's time for the next stage. Be on time, and stick to time; however, most people will give you more than ten minutes of their valuable time – but don't plan on it, and don't worry if not.

Introduce yourself, thank them in advance for giving up their time and check how much time you have for the meeting. Ask your questions about the industry, how to enter, what employers look for, any specific qualifications, what makes people success-ful, what is exciting about working there – these are genuine questions to which you really want the answers!

At the end of the meeting, make sure to ask for two more contacts that they can suggest. 'This has been incredibly useful – can you recommend anyone else I could talk to?' If you can get two names from everyone you meet, you'll soon have more connections than you can manage.

After the meeting, be sure to send a thank you note – it doesn't have to be handwritten; an email will do.

Then you can start the process again, if you are still interested after your meeting, with the contacts you have been given. These contacts will probably be strangers to you, so open your email with 'Mary Smith suggested I contact you . . .' The new contact is much more likely to open the note as they will know and respect Mary Smith. After a few meetings you may well have four, eight, sixteen contacts to follow up – at this stage you may decide not to pursue some if they are in an industry or part of the country you aren't interested in, you won't worry if some don't respond to your request, and you won't be too stressed if some can't meet for a few weeks – not only do you have your studies or current job to worry about, you probably have some other meet-ings too.

Every few months, make sure you write round to everyone you've met (your network) to let them know how you're getting on; you might want to include a link to an interesting and relevant article on the industry. Finally, when you land your next role or decide what job to take, write to them all again – success has many parents, and they all wish to congratulate you on your success that they will feel they had some part in.

## FACE-TO-FACE MEETINGS

There is a shape to face-to-face meetings, an overall arc of energy and engagement; it rises up as you get to know the other person and make some introductory comments, peaking with a long central section as you get into the body of the meeting, then turning down again as you make a warm close, confirm actions and part.

### Getting started

The first part of the meeting is to get the energy/engagement curve off the ground and building upwards – this is when you start to build rapport with the other person or people. You build rapport by listening, by finding common ground, and by pacing them. So-called 'small talk' is aimed at building rapport – and you can throw out some hooks to find the common ground. Obviously, the fact you're having the meeting is one element of common ground, but beyond that you'll look for areas of mutual interest. This could include:

★ Very neutral topics: the weather, the traffic, the view out of the window – no risk of offence here but not very insightful.
★ Promising topics: sports, positive observations about the organisation, previous connections, news items about the industry.
★ Very risky topics (that is, don't do it!): politics, religion, personal comments.

Depending on the style of meeting, the other person may have your CV and will, in an effort to warm up the meeting, ask you about your interests. This is why the bottom section of your CV, about interests, is so important. To repeat the CV section, make sure you have two or three items in the interests that gives people something to ask about; so not 'cooking' but 'been on training course for Asian cuisine, now cook Indian food twice weekly'.

## Down to business

Remind them why you are there and confirm how much time you and they have. 'I understand that we are able to meet for fifteen minutes,' for example. Demonstrate awareness, weave in your knowledge of the organisation or sector. You may have gleaned this from the web, from noticeboards, from people who work there or in the industry, and from previous meetings you've had.

Make sure you demonstrate **active listening**: you have two ears and one mouth, so make sure you use them in that proportion. Some people say you have two ears, two eyes and only one mouth – but that would have you speaking just 20 per cent of the time, which seems a bit low to me.

Anyway, active listening is showing the other person that you're really interested in what they are saying: it's not enough just to be listening and taking it all in – you must *show* the other person that you're doing that. So write notes (ideally by hand as a tablet or laptop will create a physical barrier that you don't want), nod, and summarise; for example, you might say, 'Let me just check that I've understood that correctly, did you say 250 . . .?' It shows you've been listening, making the effort to write it down and to get it right, and it also gives the other person a chance to correct or enlarge on the point.

If you have any concerns about whether you are an active listener, then video yourself and watch the result. Do you look interested? Lots of active listening signs? Sitting forward? Nodding and saying, 'uh huh'? It's worth practising, as it will make your meeting go a lot better.

And one particular example of the face-to-face meeting is the interview.

# INTERVIEWS

Whether on the phone or in person, over a video link or via a
recorded machine-interview, you'll need to do well at interviewing to get the job you want, and to work out if it is a job you really
want. I'm going to focus on face-to-face interviews, and add
some comments on differences with phone, video or online
interviews as I go along.

So what is an interview? An event in which you get to meet one
or more people who ask you questions to assess if they want to
work with you. As with all aspects of the job search, it's useful to
step into their shoes and ask what are they looking for? How will
they assess if they want to work with you? And if you knew that,
how would you show them?

First things first: you're in the room for the interview because,
based on the CV, cover letter, other forms and tests you've
completed, and maybe based on some references, they think
that, *on paper*, you could do the job. So you're well on your way.
Most people who applied have not got this far.

Let's talk through the process – one or more people will ask you
a series of questions, which may or may not be from a script, for
between fifteen minutes and an hour. The interview could be a
one-to-one meeting in a hotel lobby, in armchairs or sofas, a

one-to-two interview in a small office, or a formal office with you at the focus of a U-shaped table with seven people taking it in turns to ask you questions.

Your interviewers may be from other countries and cultures to you, and English may not be their first language. They may speak faster or slower than you; want more or less eye contact with you. If you haven't already been told, I'd recommend phoning up ahead of time to find out what to expect, how many interviews, how long, with whom (names and titles would be helpful for some background research), usual dress code in the office, and the format of the interviews.

On the day, it may all change as perhaps some people are not available and have been replaced, or a different room is being used. Don't let any of that upset or worry you – the point of this paragraph is that you need to be ready for anything; for example, someone you know is on the interview panel, there is a dog in the room, the chairs are very low, there is noisy intermittent building work in the next room, the fire alarm goes off, or some people on the panel are dressed much more or much less smartly than you.

It's probably best to avoid commenting on any elements that seem unusual or unexpected – they might well be completely usual to the other people in the room and anything you say may sound critical.

## Dress for success

What to wear probably causes the most anxiety. 'Whether on the phone, video or in person, you should dress up for an interview to show the organisation that you take the process seriously, to make yourself feel good, to send your brain the implicit signal that the interview is important, and so that you'll feel at ease during the process.

If the recruiter hasn't issued any instructions, and you haven't asked, then the rule of thumb is that it's fine to be as, or more, smartly dressed than the recruiters. So even if they wear jeans and T-shirts, wearing more formal clothes is fine. Once you have the job, you can adopt the house style of jeans and T-shirts.

And now the vexed question of what to wear. An interview is not a fashion show, a party or a date; you want the interviewers to concentrate on you, and not your fashion sense or, in their mind, perhaps your lack of fashion sense. So smart, simple and not attracting attention. For men, it's a safe bet to wear a suit (dark blue or grey – plain or some subtle pattern but not a loud check), white shirt and a nice tie. If men want to demonstrate their character, then do this through the tie – subtle, understated. For women, it's not as easy as just saying, 'suit and tie'; women can wear suits of course, but smart, work-style dresses or skirt, blouse and cardigan can work too.

Subtle jewellery is fine – but avoid the array of jangling bracelets or long dangling earrings that distract the other person (and maybe you too). Subtle perfume or aftershave if you usually wear this – but do keep it subtle. Similarly with make-up – enough to make you feel ready and confident. Polished and cared-for foot-wear is important – it demonstrates attention to detail.

Above all, make sure you are comfortable in whatever you wear. If the new shoes have given you blisters on the way to the office, you'll be distracted. Make sure you can sit down in whatever you are wearing – tight skirts might be a problem here; and if you get hot easily, or when under pressure, then dress coolly.

Needless to say (perhaps more for women than men) don't dress provocatively – no low-cut tops or mini-skirts.

Try to have coats and bags that are similarly professional. Don't go out specially to buy new ones (unless you'd like to) but don't spoil the impression with some old backpack, covered in stickers, and a favourite but tatty coat. You may not always be able to leave the coat at reception, and have to take it into the interview room with you, to hang in full view of the interviewer. Next, what might you want in the bag?

### It's in the bag – what to take to an interview
In your bag, you'll probably find it useful to have the job description and ad, a copy of your CV and application (for example, cover letter, answers to essay questions), a pen (that works, doesn't leak, and is not a freebie from a competitor of the organisation you are visiting . . . it has happened), pad of paper or notebook, a set of questions you think they might ask you, some questions that you might ask them, any background information on who you are meeting, the organisation and so on, your phone (on airplane mode or switched off so it doesn't even buzz once you are in the room), and contact details for the interview in case you are delayed.

On your way, make sure you read your CV and application letter again – you'd be surprised how many people are unable to answer questions about their CV succinctly, or worse, have forgotten what is on their CV and express surprise. Then re-read the job description. Get your points straight in your mind about the examples you will use to illustrate each element.

### Timing your arrival
In an ideal world, you'll be at reception about ten minutes before the time they want you there. If you're the sort of person to leave things to the last minute and time everything to the second, with no safety margin – then you should probably add in another chunk of time, depending on how far you have to go. A 9 a.m. start in another city fifty miles away probably means going over the night before – unless you're excited about the 6 a.m. start on the milk

train. An 11 a.m. start, a couple of miles away, probably means a leisurely breakfast reading over notes before leaving at 10 a.m.

I'd take the coach or train one earlier than the one that arrives with just ten minutes to spare; all being well you'll have time to get coffee in a nearby shop, and if there are delays, traffic jams or a breakdown, you'll be able to relax as your insurance time is used up.

Check out online maps for where you're going, and street view can prepare you for what the entrance looks like – if the organisation has several offices in the city, make sure you're going to the right one.

## Questions, questions

Your chance to shine – answering the questions they ask you with examples that show how you can do the job, take responsibility, achieve things and would be a terrific colleague for them. An interview is not an interrogation by the secret police but a two-way exchange – after all, if you turn out to be exactly who they want, and they've given you a tough grilling, then you're not likely to want to work there. An interview is a two-way process: you are also assessing them and the organisation, and whether you really want to work there.

### Your responsibility

Your job in an interview is to make sure that you have presented the best and clearest version of you, and how you could do the job.

Note that your task in an interview does not include deciding whether to offer you the role – that's their responsibility. So when the interview's over, don't worry about something that is not your concern.

Preparation is everything. Like a politician on a radio interview, make sure you know the top three facts about your skills and experience that you think will be important to the interviewer, and that you will weave into at least one answer. It's not as exaggerated as: 'I'll answer your question on the flooding situation in Ruritania in a moment, but first I want to tell you about my new plans for primary schools,' but an interview is your chance to tell them what you want them to know.

Think about the examples you're going to use – there's nothing much worse than starting out with a story from your past, and half-way through remembering that it doesn't actually end that well or show you in a good light. Nor is it very professional to say, 'Gosh, which example shall I give you? Hmmm, let me think . . . (pause) . . . OK, I'll try this one.'

You can find sets of questions for interviews in whole books dedicated to the subject, but you can come up with your own list of what you'd expect. Here are some ideas to get you started, grouped into basically the same question:

★ Why do you want the job? What attracts you to the position?
★ Why should we appoint you?
★ What are your strengths and weaknesses? What would your best friend/worst enemy say about you?
★ Which part of the job description do you think you can do immediately? Will have to learn?
★ What do you know about us? Our website? Why this organisation instead of competitors?
★ Where do you see yourself in five/ten years' time? What are your future plans?
★ If you had a magic wand, what one thing would you wish for at this organisation?
★ Here's a scenario . . . what would you do/have done?

★ Tell us about a time when you were part of a project that went wrong, and what you did about it. Tell us about a time when you disagreed with your boss and what you did.

★ Take us through your career to date, explaining why you made the choices you did.

There'll be one or two possible questions that worry you the most. Think about the question you *least* want to come up and add it to the list. It might be about a gap in your CV, about a poor exam result, a time you were made redundant, or a job that you stayed in for a very short time (a week? three months?). Everyone's human – even your interviewers – but you'll feel better if you have thought about and prepared a convincing, confident and honest explanation, for example, 'I took three months out to gather my thoughts, get healthy, move to another city, look after my partner, explore what I really wanted to do with my life.'

Ask other people for their ideas of questions you're likely to get. They've probably had interviews and can share the sorts of questions they were asked – put them all on the list.

For a phone or video interview you can have your notes out in front of you, including the key points and examples you want to communicate.

### Here's one I prepared earlier

Armed with the list of likely questions, it's time to prepare your answers. Start by thinking of the job description and what the recruiter is looking for. As well as the general points about responsibility, achievement and team player, they might have written that they are looking for, say, sales skills, graphic design, creativity, numeracy, ability to work under pressure, ability to influence others and so on. Jot these points down.

Next, consider the question list – for each question, start to draft the main points of the answer, then check off how many of the job description points are being addressed. In other words, if you're talking about your career to date, and want to stress your sales skills, you should bring out examples of sales skills you had, or wanted to develop, at each stage in your career. In the final version, this should be fairly subtle.

Most students I meet are most worried about the questions that start: 'Tell me about a time when you demonstrated teamwork/leadership/inspiration'. In your preparation, you should make sure you know exactly which examples you are going to use for each of these sorts of questions. You don't want to have to take time when you're on the spot, to think which example to choose, or worse to start saying, 'Oh, good question. Let me think. Can I tell you about X?'

Interviewers want a crisp answer, and you want to have the best example, clearly explained. So you can use STAR as a structure for answering these questions: Describe the Situation, the Task you took on, the Action you took, and the Result. I'd take about two sentences on each one. You can also add another R at the end, for Reflection. Make sure it's about 'I' not 'we'. The benefit of STAR is that you spend equal time on all the aspects to cover, and you don't miss anything out. I've seen too many candidates spend at least three minutes on setting up the situation, and forget to describe the result of what they did.

## An example of STAR

'Tell us about a time when you worked on a project that was going wrong, and what you did about it.'

Situation: 'The RAG magazine was due to be published for RAG week and two weeks before the deadline, was still not ready to go to the printers. As a committee we had planned to make £2,000 from sales, and had got some key local advertisers involved, so couldn't afford not to publish.'

Task: 'I took on the task of making sure we would deliver the magazine on time – first to get it camera-ready, to the printer, then to the distributors.'

Action: 'I gathered the team of three designers and writers and worked with them, planning in detail what we had left to do, how it could fit around their lectures, who else might be drafted in, and some day-by-day targets.'

Result: 'As a result, we got to the printers just one day late, but they really helped and it went on sale on time. We did actually raise £2,200 in the end.'

Reflection: 'Looking back, I could have saved work by reducing pages and, of course, noticing the warning bells of missed deadlines earlier.'

This answer would take about ninety seconds to say: it's succinct, focused and clear. If an interviewer wants to find out more, they can probe. For example, 'How did you motivate the team when it looked like the deadline would be missed?'

Practise some STAR stories for a few key questions that you think might be asked.

## Points not scripts

You won't want to sound over-rehearsed – and the adrenaline on the day will help that – but it's probably better to prepare by jotting down just the key points you want to bring up under each question. You'll also find it easier to remember points rather than whole scripts – and you'll need to be flexible and listen, as the questions won't be in the form or order that you have written out.

## On the day – in the moment

Your name is called and you stand up, and walk towards the interview room. The moment has arrived when you'll spend half an hour or so with an interviewer, each working out if you want to work with the other. To repeat that point – while an interview is mostly 'them' learning about you, it's also a chance for you to learn about them and to work out if they are the sort of people, and this is the sort of culture, where you'd like to spend most of your waking hours.

It's an old cliché that people make up their mind about someone new they meet within fifteen seconds, and there is some research that supports this view. Malcolm Gladwell's book, *Blink: The Power of Thinking without Thinking*, asserts that it is an essential part of being human, to 'thin slice' the information and experience you collect about someone in just a few seconds, and goes on to show that it can be quite an accurate assessment.

Given the interviewer may have made an initial assessment of you before you have even sat down, what can you do to make that first impression really good? First, given people will be 'reading' you, it's advisable to give as much information as possible by being open and expressive, smiling and warm. Second, identify things that you have in common to play to the 'similarity attraction hypothesis' wherein we all have a reflex of being attracted to people who are similar to us. This is where the Interest section of your CV comes into play – *not* that you need to have played specific sports, or had some particular interest – more that you have described some activity, in a little detail, that the interviewer can latch on to and talk about.

Hear the music.

As you walk into the room, in those critical first few seconds, hear the trumpets play in your head to announce your arrival. Walk in firmly and confidently, smile, make eye contact and, if appropriate, give a good handshake. Sit when (and where) invited; sit firmly on the whole seat, but with your mind on the front; sit up, don't slump and do not, unlike a candidate I once interviewed, put your feet up on the desk. Breathe. If there is more than one person, look at each one and smile as you are introduced.

**Handshake**

First recorded in the sixth century BC, the handshake is thought to be a demonstration that neither party is holding a weapon. Not that that is usually an issue in an interview. A good handshake can make the difference so don't ignore it: firm and full (that is, right into the web between thumb and forefinger). Look the other person in the eye when shaking hands.

It's not a demonstration of wills, so don't crush the other person's hand, nor imitate a wet fish by offering a clammy or limp hand. If you've travelled to the interview, and have arrived early, take time to wash and dry your hands.

## Strengths-based interviews

More jargon for an apparently new form and style of interviewing candidates, but underneath it's still trying learn if you could do the job well, and 'fit' in the organisation. And they do this with so-called 'strengths-based interviews' – asking you to describe what you enjoy doing – the hypothesis being that if you work at something you really enjoy and are good at, you'll enter a state of *flow*, a psychological term for those activities where you are fully immersed and completely absorbed, perhaps losing track of time, and performing at your best – something employers rather like.

The other argument in favour of these style of questions, or finding a work environment that plays to your strengths, is that you would automatically be happier working there.

**Strengths versus deficits**

A strength-based approach to interviewing appears to have transferred from the world of social work, where it was seen as a challenge to the opposite, that is 'deficit-focus', and arose around 1999. It is worth noting that there is insufficient evidence to demonstrate that such an approach is effective.

Strengths type questions might be:

★ What do you enjoy doing?
★ What are your greatest weaknesses (and/or strengths)?
★ When are you most yourself?
★ What is usually left until last on your To Do list?

In reality, you can expect a mixture of strengths-based and competency questions in the same interview. Like all interviews, if you've prepared by thinking what sort of questions you're going to be asked, then you won't need to fret over what type of interview you're going to encounter.

## CASE STUDY INTERVIEWS

One particular type of interview, an especial favourite of 'City' employers like management consultancies, investment banks and others, is the case study. The good news is that you can learn to do cases well: if you don't practise at all, and decide to wing it, then it is pretty unlikely to be that successful.

Like all interviews, the case study is an exercise for the interviewer to work out if they want you on their team. Key things they'll look for are: do you take control of the case? Do you own it? Have you got a structured way of approaching the case? Are you aware of all the different ways to answer the question? Do you involve the interviewer in *helping* solve the case?

The structure is that you will be asked a business-type question and asked how you would approach solving it. You may spend ten to thirty minutes on the case, gradually getting into more detail – unwrapping the onion, layer by layer. In my view, questions fall into two basic groups:

1. We have a historic problem and want to understand the causes and correct it – this could include: profits have fallen, or market share has dropped, or we can't meet customer demand.
2. We want to do something new – this could include: we want to enter a new geographic market, or introduce a new product or service, or buy a competitor.

### Overall structure for a case study

A case study is a mirror of a consultancy project, so if you find you don't really like this way of working, it might be telling you that you're not really cut out for consulting. When posed a question, as one consulting firm puts it, 'Do you want the three-minute, three-day, three-week or three-month answer?' You're there to give the 'three-minute' answer – but the structure is the same: from Structure to Hypotheses, to Data/Evidence required to prove the hypotheses, to Conclusions and Recommendations.

The last point, recommendations, is vital; clients pay consultants to *recommend* what to do, not just explain why things have gone wrong. If, for example, the interviewer asks you to think about the issues to consider when setting up a new coffee shop, you could go through four steps – remembering to show your workings by writing things on the paper on the table between you, and by thinking out loud:

1. Structure:
   'I'd want to consider factors such as price, services, products, location, competitors, and customers. I may have some more in a minute, but I'll start with these.'
2. Hypotheses:
   'My hypotheses for each of these factors are: if we offer more services, we'll attract more customers; there is limited competition, especially at certain times of day; the most lucrative market is mothers and toddlers/script writers/ students . . .' (and so on for all the parts of the structure).
3. Data:
   'To prove or disprove these hypotheses, I'd survey the competitors by visiting each existing coffee shop in the target area, noting down prices, services, numbers of customers, atmosphere, opening hours and so on. I might go at different times of day to collect data.'
4. Conclusions and Recommendations:
   'If we found that most coffee shops close at 5 p.m., and that there is demand (from our surveys) for evening service, I would recommend exploring the costs and benefits of opening until 8 p.m., 10 p.m. and even midnight.'

You should aim to take control and 'own' the problem so get through all of step 1, structuring the problem (which could take two to three minutes uninterrupted) before you stop and perhaps ask, 'Are there any of these that you'd like me to start with in generating hypotheses?'

Keep writing out the points as you go along, sketch some graphs and charts with made-up information to illustrate the point; it's a great 'leave behind' after the meeting and a useful tool for you to draw your interviewer in to a conversation. They can follow your argument and structure more easily, and can start to point things out until it genuinely becomes a two-way discussion of a shared problem.

## A digression on estimating

Along the way, you may be asked to make some arithmetic estimates just to see how adept you are with mental arithmetic – occasionally these might be separate questions or even 'brain teasers'. Examples of these are: why are manhole covers round? How heavy is this building? How long would it take to move Mount Fuji? How many golf balls fit in a jumbo jet?

The point of these exercises is to see if you can make a reasonable estimate of the sizes of common things – the diameter of a golf ball, the length or weight or seat capacity of an aeroplane, or the population of London. For example, you may never have played golf but you're pretty sure that a golf ball is bigger than 10mm and smaller than 1m; in fact, having put an upper and lower boundary on it, you can probably reduce the range to, say between 30mm and 100mm, and for now choose a mid-point of 60mm. (It's actually 42.7mm for a US ball, and 41.1mm for a British ball – so there's no universal standard anyway.)

It doesn't matter that your estimate is just that, an estimate – the point is that you made it, it's the right order of magnitude (that is, not millimetres or metres but tens of millimetres), and that it's to one significant figure (that is, 60 not 62.345). Given that you want to show how you take control of the case, even one as simple as this, do *not* say, 'Well, I've never played golf, have no idea how big a golf ball is – tell me, how big is a golf ball?' Do say, 'Hmm, a golf ball – [holding up hand and moving thumb and forefinger towards and away from each other in a pinching motion until they are about a golf ball diameter apart] – so, what's that? I'm going to go with an estimate of 6cm, which is 60mm.'

If you're estimating how many golf balls fit in St Paul's Cathedral (or a jumbo jet, or the room you are in) then I'd also suggest you stick to the same units – and metric is easier than imperial, unless you love dividing cubic inches into cubic yards . . .

### AN EXAMPLE OF AN ESTIMATE

For an estimating question like 'How much ice cream is eaten in Britain each year?' the best candidates will try one method, and then try a *second,* different, method to compare estimates. So the first method might be, 'I eat about a tub a month, so that's about a litre each month, but not so much in winter so total for the year might be 10 litres. Assuming I'm representative, multiply 10 litres a year by 60 million people in Britain and you get 600 million litres a year. I suppose children eat more than me and older people eat much less than me, so my estimate of 10 litres a year each may be high.'

Then the best candidate will continue, 'Now a second way to think of this is volumes sold, in cafés and restaurants, through mobile vans, and through supermarkets. First, taking cafés – there are three in my city of 150,000 residents that specialise in ice cream. We could estimate how much each sells every day based on, say, 10 hours a day x 20 servings per hour x 200 ml per serving = 80 litres a day from one café. Eighty litres a day is approximately 24,000 litres a year x 3 cafés in this city (plus other places such as restaurants), say 100,000 litres a year – and if my city is representative then Britain is 400 x the population of this city (= 60,000,000 divided by 150,000) – so total volume sold in British cafés and restaurants is 400 x 100,000 = 40 million litres.

'Next, I'll add on the same volume again for ice cream sold by vans and by supermarkets to get a total second estimate of 80 million litres.' Your two estimates will probably be quite different but they would give you a range: 'My estimate for ice cream eaten in Britain each year is between 80 million and 600 million litres.'

## ASSESSMENT CENTRES
Not content with your academic qualifications, your CV, your cover letter, a face-to-face interview and maybe some online or written tests, many recruiters feel they'd like you to take part in what can be called an assessment centre. These can range from half a day to three days, consist of some more case studies and examples, include physical exercises (if it's Sandhurst's assessment for the army). For most people, though, an assessment centre really is an employer trying to mimic a real job to see how you'll cope – and to do it for long enough that you can't keep faking it.

I once worked with a Human Resources manager who told me that interviews should be longer than half an hour, because if someone really is faking something, they can only do it for thirty minutes. Whether that's true or not, it doesn't matter to you because you won't be faking anything, or putting on any act. If you did, and you got the job, well, then you'd have to act like that for the rest of your career at that organisation. Not a great idea for how you'll spend most of your waking hours.

Recruiters will have designed their exercises at an assessment centre to see if you're capable of those key skills such as team working, communicating, listening, problem solving, and influencing. All those skills you learned at nursery – playing nicely in the sandpit together with the others – well, they're going to pay off here. (You *did* play nicely, didn't you?) Let's first discuss the main type of formal assessment: group exercises.

## GROUP EXERCISES – HOW YOU PLAY THE GAME

There's no winning or losing in a group exercise but what you are being assessed on is how you play. You'll be put in a group of other applicants (anywhere from two to twelve, but most likely six to eight) and given a task to complete as a group within a fixed time. One or more people will be observing you the entire time, though some observers may be invisible to you. The task might range from being very specific: 'Here are some sales and cost data for a new product; what should the company do, given the performance?' to very non-specific: 'Decide on a topic and reach a conclusion.'

Observers are there to watch and record your actions and behaviour during the session – so be sure to give them something to observe. But not too much. So do join in and don't dominate by doing all the talking.

You can join in, even when you can't think of anything that you think is useful, by bringing other people in, especially those who maybe haven't read this book and are being too quiet. 'X, what do you think about this?' Bringing other people in is a really important role (in real life too!) and goes down well with assessors. With those who have joined in and contributed, build on their ideas and praise them too. 'That's a really good idea, and if we combined that with what X said over here a few minutes ago, I wonder whether you all think we should consider doing Y?'

Keep an eye on the clock, but don't over-manage this: 'OK, I think we've got about five minutes left, shall we try to get some of these great ideas down on paper?' It's likely that the assessors will have left you flip charts, pens, maybe a computer, and other visual aids. In a short time period, stick to just pen and paper – be aware that if you do volunteer to be 'scribe' you may end up standing up at the flip chart, away from the group (sitting round the table), and finding it difficult to still contribute ideas while writing other people's suggestions. One way round this, if you really can't resist getting the team's ideas on paper – and it looks like no one else is doing this – is to bring a piece of flip chart paper to the team table so everyone can join in, you stay physically in the group, and don't get stuck with trying to listen, write, edit, arbitrate, and contribute all at the same time.

Try not to have pride in ownership; if the group don't initially want to run with your patently obviously brilliant idea, then don't force the issue. The group comes first and you're trying to show what a good team player you are, and second, your brilliant idea may come up again, perhaps in a different form, a few minutes later – maybe from someone else, or maybe from you gently trying one more time.

## TRIAL BY SHERRY

As well as the formal exercises, there may be an informal assessment of you, over some form of socialising – this might be over lunch with other applicants and many members of the recruiting organisation, and/or over dinner the night before or after, so called *Trial by Sherry*. More assessment of whether you'll be a great member of the team, are you good to have around? Do remember that this part is definitely two-way – a great chance for you to assess them, would you like to be in their team? Would you look forward to getting up in the morning and working at that organisation? Does it satisfy your key objectives for a job, for example, intellectual challenge, working with like-minded, stimulating people, doing something worthwhile, and so on?

## PRESENTATIONS

'We'd like your interview to start with a ten-minute presentation by you of: "Issues affecting the doughnut business". You can use PowerPoint if you like; there will be an audience of eight.'

If such an invitation throws you into a panic, then you are not alone. Most people do not welcome the idea of standing up in front of others to make a presentation; it makes them nervous and concerned about their performance. Other times when you may have to give a presentation include at an assessment centre at the end of a team exercise, or in a pre-prepared case study where you've been given time to review the information and have to present your conclusions.

The overall aim of your presentation is to *entertain* the audience. Entertain means to engage them, draw them in so they want to listen, show them why they will benefit from listening. If they are enjoying the presentation, they will engage, sit up, listen, take notes, ask questions, and generally feel that the time has been valuably spent.

Think back on all the presentations you have been to, be they at school or college, in work or outside, by recruiters or on TV. Think about what makes a good experience at the theatre or cinema. You remember two overall parts: the person giving the presentation and some of the content.

### All about you . . .

Like a great actor, you want the audience's eyes on you, not on your slides, or notes you've handed out. By the time you give your presentation, you will know your content inside out; so you'll only use slides and notes to give structure and to illustrate information that can't be easily described, for example, maps, photographs, cartoons, or diagrams.

Just as in an interview, the audience is deciding whether you are someone they want to work with: are you open and honest? Warm and empathic? On top of your material? Confident (but not overconfident)? Given they make their first impression within thirty seconds, you'll want to get off to a good start – which is why you smile and, if this comes naturally, you might use a light-hearted comment so the audience smile or laugh and immediately are on your side. Such a comment does have to be in character, so if it's not your nature, don't worry, but some kind of remark that seeks out common ground can work.

As you talk, make sure you have eye contact with individuals, on one side of the room while you deliver a phrase or two, then switching to the other side. It's an interesting phenomenon that actors use in the theatre: if the audience see you making direct eye contact with one of their number, rather than gazing widely and non-specifically, then they each feel that you have connected directly with them.

Don't worry if you're not getting a strong reaction; it would be nice if they are actively listening, nodding, taking notes, sitting forward and so on – but if they are only watching in a somewhat neutral way, just keep going. They are still taking in what you are saying and how you are presenting, and probably trying to treat each candidate the same.

Do take along one or more printed copies of your slides; you can give them to the audience to make it easy for them to jot down notes and remember the presentation.

### . . . And also about the content

First, do you need PowerPoint or Keynote slides for your talk? If it's a five-minute talk, to a panel of three people, then you may decide that slides would be too distracting – remember you want them looking at you. Perhaps a simple hand-out on one or two pages of A4, or a flip chart page or two, would be appropriate. But for the ten-minute talk to eight people on 'Issues in the doughnut business', then some slides would be helpful. Not least because you can have some pictures of doughnuts and the competition.

Some tips to make your content and slides great:

★ Plan on one slide a minute, so no more than thirty slides for a half-hour presentation. Fewer than thirty would be fine, but not so few (for example, four) that the audience is distracted and bored rigid by the same slide on the screen behind you for ten minutes.
★ Keep your background really simple – a plain colour is good, you can't go wrong with black text on a white background, but you could try white text on black and so on.
★ Use the slide to show content that would be difficult or take too long to describe – for example, photos, maps, graphs.
★ Make the text legible – one target is to make the font size the average age of the audience – although this can be difficult for labels on charts.
★ No fancy fonts – something really clear and simple.
★ Fewer words the better – remember you don't want to be reading out slides. For example, if you are writing some bullet points, aim for three to five on the page, with three to six words for each. There will be exceptions but remember that brevity adds power.
★ Avoid distracting animation – a little can be good, but don't have words flying in with sound effects otherwise the audience will be getting excited about which animation you're going to use next.

★ Remember the audience will read ahead – that's good for an agenda or contents slide, but not good for one where you spend a lot of time on the first point, and they've read down the slide. So have just one main idea per slide.

★ Vary the content – text, photos, charts, quotations, maps.

## Presence

You can exude confidence by having *presence*: talk loudly and clearly enough to just fill the room – not too much so you are shouting, nor too quietly. Not too fast, and not too slowly either. Stand generally still, though not rigidly fixed to the spot. Don't cross your legs – a very common practice I've seen with women students – it sends a very strong message of fear: it makes you look as if you are trying to protect yourself from attack. Do move your arms to emphasise your points – so-called paralinguistics. You may well be tempted to have the slide clicker in one hand, and a sheaf of notes in the other (but do staple them together, and number the pages); this will limit your movements and distract your audience who may start to play the game of, 'Will they drop the pages when they try to turn them over?'

One way to avoid the sheaf of papers or cards in your hand is to know your subject – and rehearse the talk, especially if you are going to be limited in time. I wouldn't try to memorise it; you could easily forget your lines and dry up, and it could sound stilted and disengaged. There will be enough clues on each page to remind you of the points to cover – and really don't worry if you miss something. If it wasn't on the page then it will have been a detail and might be covered in the Q&A session at the end.

Please do not put your hands in your pockets, talk to the screen – or indeed anywhere except the audience – or read out the slides. If you try the last of these, the audience has no choice but to read along with you and, if you miss out or add the odd word, it will frustrate the audience even more.

When you bring up a slide that has a complex graph or chart on it, make sure you 'clear the news' from the slide first. You might say something like, 'This slide shows the relationship between number of customers, plotted on the vertical, or "y" axis, and month of the year, plotted along the horizontal, or "x" axis. The size of the circles represents the customer revenues in each month, and the colours represent each of the four geographic regions.' Having explained your graph (this one had four variables) you can now go on in your presentation to answer the 'So what?' question.

At the end of the presentation, you can ask for questions: 'Thank you for listening; I'll now be happy to take any questions.' Then stop, and wait. If it's a big audience, who don't know each other, then this really is a matter of someone breaking the ice – after the first question, more tend to flood in. It's very good practice if you can repeat a question that's been asked, perhaps rephrased, so that all the audience hear it. You could rephrase if you wanted to remove the emotion from a question, or just to demonstrate that you've understood it, or to explain any jargon or abbreviations that perhaps some of the audience might not understand. 'The question was whether there is any connection between advertising spend and customer sales.'

When you answer the question, keep your eye contact with different people, and make sure you finish your answer looking at someone other than the questioner – otherwise the questioner may feel that they can come back with another question.

### Overall structure
Tell them what you're going to tell them, tell them, and then tell them what you told them.

At best, audiences remember three things from your presentation (though mostly they remember your body language, voice, style, and whether they enjoyed it). Work out what the three (or fewer) key messages are, and focus your talk on just these.

After a title slide, with your name on it, your next slide will be the agenda. If you're limited in the number of slides you can use, then merge the title and the agenda slides.

'In this talk, I'm going to describe the current situation, the three key issues the organisation faces, and make two recommendations to address those issues.'

Next slide(s) will describe the current situation – some charts, graphs, photos, text and so on. Then a set of slides on those three key issues (probably one per slide), and finally the slides with your recommendations. Final slide is to tell them what you've just told them, 'To summarise, the situation at XYZ is . . . , the three key issues that XYZ faces are A, B and C, and two recommendations to consider are D and E.'

Once you have more than, say, ten slides, help the audience understand where you are in the presentation. You can do this in several ways:

★ Repeat the agenda slide at each change of section, highlighting the new section, with a box or colour.
★ Number the slides and tell the audience how many there are at the beginning: 'I'm going to speak for about ten minutes and run through twelve slides during the talk.'
★ Have small labels on each slide, for example, in the top left-hand corner, showing the section. In the above example, you might have 'Key issues' in the top left of the three slides about the key issues.

**Structure for each page**

Think about the story you are telling (everyone likes stories, after all) to choose the main points to get across. When you get to each page, attract the audience's attention by telling them why the page is important. Think of this like a newspaper – headline at the top to attract attention, then unwrap the story.

★ Write a headline at the top that states something important and to which the audience cannot say 'So what?' An example: 'Sales were $1 million in 2015' would fail this test, 'Sales of $1 million in 2015 were 20 per cent lower than the prior year due to tough competition' has the audience sitting up and taking notice. Not only have you put the sales number in context, but it doesn't sound a good result, and you're introducing a possible reason for the situation.

★ The content of the page should support the headline so that if the audience wants to challenge your strong message, you have the evidence. That evidence can be text (for example, bullet points), or a chart, or a photograph or perhaps some combination of these.

## NEGOTIATING THE OFFER

You've passed the interviews, the assessment centre, made the presentation and done the online tests, and after an anxious few days, you get the email or phone call offering you the job. All done? Not at all, as now is your strongest moment to negotiate. What you can negotiate now sets the starting point for all future pay rises, and the tone in your relationship. If you think that annual pay rises might be based on a fixed percentage, then you'd want your starting salary to start high. However, you also want to leave some room at the top of the range so you're not under intense pressure to justify your salary from Day 1 in the job.

There is some research recently that claimed that the reason women can be paid less than men for the same job is that men negotiate more when they take the job, whereas women can be more accepting of the first offer.

Whatever the cause, don't accept the first offer you are made, but do acknowledge it. I've met students who say, 'I received this job offer a week ago, and I don't really know what to do so I've just ignored it for now.' Wrong. When you get the offer, respond warmly and promptly, make sure you understand all the details of the offer, and ask for some time to consider it (even if just overnight). No one will criticise you for that.

## DETAILS, DETAILS

Do get the details of the offer in writing, particularly all the fringe benefits. Not just the salary, but any sign-on bonus, private medical plan, free meals at work, dry cleaner on site – you name it. Ask about pay reviews, are they annual, biannual, when they feel like it, automatic, or never? And what is performance based on?

When do they want you to start? And where will you be working? Do you understand their expectations of your travel? Or normal working hours? Is there Time Off In Lieu ('TOIL') for working overtime or on weekends?

## ART OF NEGOTIATION

There are three key parts of negotiation: make sure you know the whole list of items the other side has, turn fixed elements into variable elements, and ask for more than you would settle at. Before you start, determine your 'BATNA' – what Fisher and Ury defined in their book *Getting to Yes: Negotiating Agreement Without Giving In* as your 'Best Alternative To a Negotiated Agreement', in other words, if we can't reach an agreement then what is my best alternative. When it's to do with a job offer, you may have a specific salary in mind: 'I just won't do it for less than £X'. If you can't negotiate the offer higher than your minimum, you'll walk away because your best alternative is better (perhaps it's take a different job, keep looking, stay where you are, do further study).

Get the full list from the recruiter about the deal on offer, decide what you like and would accept (or is not important to you). The main variable will be the pay; even if they use fixed scales (for example, universities, health service, public sector), there may be flexibility in where you are on the scale. If the salary you have been offered is a problem for you, then see what else can be varied – more training perhaps, an earlier than usual pay review (for example, after six months rather than annual), a travel card loan, some sort of success bonus, more holiday?

If they suggest a salary, then you can (and probably should) ask for more. 'Thank you for the offer of £22,000 a year basic salary but I was aiming for more than that, especially if I'm going to be living in London.'

They will most probably respond by asking what you want; if you are forced to give a number, then think of what you'd be happy with, and add more. In the above example, you might have been aiming for £24,000 and be really pleased with £25,000. So you could steel yourself and say, 'I had a range of £27,000–£28,000 in mind. I've looked at comparable organisations and roles in London and that does seem to be the going rate.' Then stop talking.

### Hurry up and wait
Silence is a powerful negotiating tool as generally people are uncomfortable with silences and will start talking to fill them. The silence may only last five seconds, but that can feel like a very long time. Try it.

> Sometimes it is essential that you sit on your hands and just wait for the other side.

Try hard not to negotiate against yourself. If they respond with, 'Hmm, that's quite high, what would you accept?' just repeat your previous range – the ball is in their court.

The first party in a negotiation to specify a number is in the weaker role. So try hard to have them start first. Recently, a student reported that the company she'd interviewed with had offered her the job and asked her, 'What salary did you have in mind?' This is really difficult so I'd advised her to ask them to bid first. If they wouldn't, then she'd have had no choice but to do some research of comparable jobs, find out the range, add some to the range, and start high.

## LUXURY OF CHOICE

Sometimes students will have two job offers, maybe more, and want help deciding which to take. Or final-year students may be deciding between further study (a Masters or a Ph.D.) and a job offer.

If you are in this luxurious position, and genuinely can't decide, then you may want to jot down all the pros and cons of each role: job content, culture of the organisation, colleagues, brand, role, location, job title, hours, expectations, prospects, what you'll learn, skills you'll acquire and so on. Test each role to see if it is opening your choices or reducing them; think about what the job after this one, in a couple of years' time, would or could be.

I've found that after ten minutes talking with a student about apparently equal offers that they really know themselves which one they want and are seeking to discuss it with someone impartial. By all means discuss it with your friends and family, but recognise that they are all emotionally invested in you and will have some biases that may not always be in your best interest.

In the end, if you still can't decide, toss a coin. Still like the answer?

# PART THREE

# Along the way, or how to keep going

## PERSEVERANCE

In Part One, I suggested you were in a helicopter at 10,000 feet above your map, getting the lie of the land and overall direction in which you wanted to travel. In Part Two, you landed and started off across the map, having Information Interviews to learn more about jobs, finding jobs to apply for, writing great CVs and cover letters, going to interviews and assessment centres, giving presentations, getting a job, and finally negotiating the offer. If only it were so straightforward; what I haven't talked about yet is that the map is not quite so benign, friendly, and supportive as I've made out so far.

With a nod to *The Pilgrim's Progress* or *The Lord of the Rings*, *The Hunger Games* or *Beowulf*, on your map there are dead ends and high walls you'll run into, thick undergrowth that will hold you back, dragons that will undermine your efforts, tempting paths that lead nowhere, and wizards who will distract you. As well, you may get tired and be ground down by a lack of instant success, and you may be rejected even though you were clearly the best candidate for the job. You may run into the powerful and invisible forces of prejudice, that are very unfair and personally wounding – be it prejudice against your race, sex, age, sexual preference, marital status, family situation, education, or background. It's not all negative: you may find, or seek out, a mentor who can advise you, or a sponsor who can help you.

This section is about the problems you may run into as you cross your career map, and how to recognise them for what they are, how to cope with them, and how to get help. I hope you don't meet all these problems, and not all at once, but you may hit some – and then this section might provide comfort and some tools to cope with and overcome them.

## WHAT'S THE WORST THAT COULD HAPPEN?

We were talking about Information Interviewing, how useful it can be for learning about industries, practising discussing your plans and background, and expanding your network.

'Probably the most effective way to arrange a meeting is to phone someone,' I was saying to the second-year student opposite me, 'or send an email to introduce yourself and offer to call a couple of days later to follow up.'

There was a pause. He was evidently uncomfortable with something I'd said.

'I could just email,' he suggested.

'Yes, you could, but it's not usually as effective. If you phone them, what's the worst thing that could happen?'

The light dawned. 'Ah yes,' he said, 'they put the phone down, don't take the call, refuse to speak to me, or do speak to me and just say No.'

Hurt feelings from being rejected are about the worst thing from this, and, even then, it doesn't reflect well on the other person. If you are about to make some cold calls, or even slightly warm calls to follow up some emails or other introductions, then it might help if you have a script prepared, or go through the likely answers and how you will react.

For example, suppose the student's phone call got the following reaction:
Executive:     'I'm sorry, I just can't talk to you.'

| | |
|---|---|
| Student: | 'I understand; is this a bad time? You have been highly recommended and if possible I would like to talk to you; could you suggest when might be a better time?' |
| Executive: | 'Oh, I don't know – I'm just up to my eyes at the moment.' |
| Student: | 'Quite understand; rather than take any more of your time now, can I arrange something with your assistant?' |
| Executive (warming up): | 'Oh, all right, but I warn you, it won't be a for a few weeks.' |
| Student: | 'That suits me, I've got my dissertation to finish. Look forward to talking in a few weeks.' |

'What's the worst that can happen?' can often be enough of a challenge to unlock your actions. Expanding the scenario described above to a bigger area, such as what if you don't get this job you are going for? What if you leave school, university or your current job, with nothing to go to next? What if you had to leave this city to follow your partner across the country? What if this employer made your position redundant and you (like many others) lost your job?

Voicing the worst possible outcome can be liberating. You acknowledge that this dark thing, which has been lurking in the back of your mind, might happen. Defining it and talking about it, first just to yourself, and then with other people, can be an important step in thinking and planning how to manage it, if it were to happen.

I was once consulting with an arts organisation. One morning, we challenged the management team with the question: What if the organisation lost 20 per cent of its funding? In those days, this was quite a realistic scenario; while everyone hoped it wouldn't happen they did agree that it was important to plan ahead for a large drop in income, before it actually came to pass.

As the morning progressed, everyone reviewed their activities and the money they spent. A typical and recurring comment was, 'I suppose this activity hasn't been as effective as we thought, we could stop doing it.' After an hour or two, we had a long list of activities and projects that could be stopped if the money wasn't there; I would guess that most of them were discretionary but some were important and precious to the organisation and were last on the list.

We then posed a different question: What if the organisation gained 20 per cent more funding? The mood in the room brightened up – 'Ah, now, we could really get going on new ideas and creative projects we've wanted to do for a long time.' A list quickly emerged, the team was excited; however, where was the extra money to come from?

'You've already found the money,' I observed. 'The first part of the morning uncovered projects that you feel you could stop with no major impact, certainly not the impact that these new projects might have – and, what's more important, you're all much more energised about these new ideas.'

How does this story apply to you and your career? You don't have to look at the very worst situation, but you could challenge yourself by changing some elements: what if my salary went down 50 per cent? What if we had to move house? What if I needed more qualifications or skills?

### 'No' doesn't mean never

Along the way, you will (I'm afraid to say) meet rejection whether that is for a carefully written job application you wrote, a phone call asking for advice, or not progressing from the assessment centre to the next round of interviews. So be it, we learn more from our failures than from our successes.

But, it may not be a failure. Fundraisers are taught (for example, by Bernard Ross of the Management Centre) that when they ask people for money, and receive 'No' for an answer, they should treat it that in only one of nine cases does that mean 'Go away for ever'.

I think that you can apply what fundraisers have learned to your own career path across the map – when someone says 'No' to you, what does it really mean? Here are eight examples of when 'No' doesn't mean never, with my explanation:

★ Not now – This is an inconvenient time (I'm just rushing off to a meeting) or this is the wrong time (we're not hiring at the moment, next month looks better).
★ Not this exactly – We like you, you have some interesting skills, but this opportunity is not exactly for you, we're looking for different skills or experience.
★ Not you – With fundraisers this means that the potential funder wants to talk to someone else. As a job seeker, you'll want to find out what it is about you that the person doesn't gel with; you could offer to introduce someone else if you can think of anyone who is more appropriate (once you know what that is).
★ Not me – I'm the wrong person to answer your questions
★ Not unless – You'll have to provide more information, do something else, meet me at Heathrow, or send me a CV, for me to agree to what you're asking.
★ Not in this way – I don't do face-to-face meetings, or email, or Skype calls.
★ Too much – You're asking for too much time or information.
★ Too little – You're not asking me for enough, I'm not interested in just chatting about information about this industry, when I'm trying to hire new staff.

All of these 'No's, with the extra information, are not actually 'No', and can help you change your request to get a 'Yes'. The challenge you may have is if the person just says, 'No', without the helpful extra bit about 'not now' or 'not me'. You must, therefore, deploy your listening skills to the fore – and not be put off by an initial 'No'. You might try to help them with suggestions:

'When you say "No", is there some specific reason why not? Is now a bad time? Or you'd rather meet in a different way (phone/Skype/face-to-face)?'

Then be quiet. Let them fill the silence.

Assuming it's one of the eight not-never versions of 'No', then you can respond showing some flexibility.

'I understand you don't think you're the right person, who would you recommend I speak to?' (open question) not, 'Is there a colleague I could speak to?' (closed question) as you'll risk getting another 'No'.

In a way, you're trying to do what sales people call *closing the deal*. There are several ways to close a deal, but one that you might find useful here is the *assumptive* close, giving the person two choices, and not mentioning the third, which is, do nothing. For example, 'I understand you're really busy now, I'll call you next week when things are quieter, would you prefer Wednesday or Friday morning?' (the third unspoken choice is 'or not at all?')

It can be very hard at this stage for someone to say, 'not at all'; what they might say is that neither Wednesday nor Friday are any good, but Thursday would work.

The last example of 'No' – you're not asking for enough – can catch us all out; you have one agenda that you think is achievable, maybe even a little bit challenging, and then the other person takes the lid off and wants to talk about something much bigger.

Fundraisers (again) have a list of things to ask for, and you'll have seen this on donation forms: '£5 buys clean water for a family for a day, £50 buys clean water for a week . . . £500 buys clean water for ten families for a week . . . up to £5 million buys permanent clean water for a village.' That way, if they think the person they are talking to only has £50 and it turns out they have £5000, then the fundraiser is ready.

Likewise, you need to be ready with your shopping list just in case someone asks you the dream question, 'What could you do for our business with a marketing budget of £1 million?', or some such. The chance of this happening may be low, but if it happens, you want to be ready.

## HARNESS THE UNCONSCIOUS MIND

'Where do you see yourself in five years' time?' is one of those perennial interview questions that is difficult to answer and not really obvious as to what the interviewer is looking for. It is, however, a great question for you, and if you can get some sort of view of where you see yourself, it can act as one of the strongest forces for your unconscious mind.

Without getting too mystical about it, your unconscious mind can help you achieve your three- or five-year plan, guiding you towards your goal and away from distractions. Note we say *un*conscious not *sub*conscious, since we'd like to think that the unconscious mind is of equal power to your conscious mind.

How to harness the unconscious mind? First, answer the question – when you are asked where you see yourself in the future, it doesn't really mean precisely what job title or organisation (though if you can be that precise, it can help), it means: what sort of work, type of organisation, team members, skills, experience, location, family situation; in other words, what will it feel like?

Try to answer the question when you are relaxed, on holiday, in the pub, with close friends. This is the sort of question that requires so-called 'blue sky' thinking, 'out of the box' – think wide and high, and pay no attention to any constraints (you can add those back later). You might come up with: 'I see myself running my own outdoor holiday business', 'Being a professor in a prestigious university, teaching students and researching a topic dear to my heart', or 'Leading the running of an international aid agency, making a significant difference to the lives of people in real distress'.

If there are any real constraints, and make sure they really are constraints, blend them into your three- to five-year aim.

Second, write down your aim, however difficult it may seem today, and put it away somewhere, in the back of a drawer. Get even more committed by telling someone about your aims. Now, having set your unconscious a mission, forget about the piece of paper.

Over the next few months, you may start to get ideas that are in line with your aims – I have no evidence for this but I think your unconscious has gone to work and, when you allow its ideas through, will be giving you ideas of who to call, what meeting to go to, which project to focus on, and what new skills to acquire. It also has a way of steering you away from people or opportunities that are not obviously on the path.

You may find it helpful to distract your conscious mind just enough, to let the great ideas and suggestions bubble through. One way to do this is to find a physical activity that needs some but not all your attention. I think the reason many people say they have their best ideas in the bath or shower is because they need to engage some of but not their entire conscious mind, leaving their unconscious to bubble through. Other activities might be washing up, cutting the grass, running, and ironing – all examples where you would need to concentrate but not require *all* your conscious mind.

## ARE YOU SURE? HOW DO YOU KNOW THAT?

'I'm not going to apply for that, because I'm pretty sure you have to have a certain grade or studied a specific subject,' can often be a comment from a student when discussing specific programmes or opportunities.

'Really?' I'd say. 'Are you sure? How do you know?'

'Well, everyone knows', or 'My lecturer told me', or 'My friend told me'.

They may well be right but it would be disappointing if they were wrong, perhaps because they were out-of-date or it was just rumour anyway. It can be easy to just go with the flow about what you 'know' employers are looking for, or the process you have to go through, in the heat of the moment, or when you're making many applications. So the point of this section is to suggest that you take a moment to challenge or check your understanding.

If you were an academic researcher, you'd be citing your references to support the statements you made in an essay or report; I'm suggesting that sometimes you need to act like your own researcher and make sure you can back up all the claims you are making about the way to apply, or what sort of jobs you can apply for, and so on.

Questions you might ask include:

★ Are these the only routes to becoming a lawyer?
★ Do you have to be an investment banker before going into Private Equity?
★ Can I go back to academia after industry?
★ And back again from academia to industry?

★ Or combine academic research and industry jobs?

★ Or link my academic research to an industry?

★ Must I go into management consulting immediately?

★ Must I get a PGCE to be a schoolteacher?

★ Do I have to take an unpaid internship to get anywhere in heritage/media/marketing?

★ Must I start at the bottom of a charity/NGO if I want to be in a senior role in five to ten years' time?

Why should you check? Because routes change; the professions open up, exams change, courses change, companies emerge and others close. Consider teaching: ten or more years ago, most people wanting to be teachers enrolled on a PGCE (Post Graduate Certificate in Education) course, and a few joined an independent school without having a PGCE. Now, you can join TeachFirst, get six weeks' training and be in a school the same year; or you can join SchoolsDirect, and start working and training in a set of local state schools straight away; or you can join an Academy chain of schools and start teaching and being trained; or join an independent school and start teaching and study for a part-time PGCE – and those are just the main routes, with more opening up each year. So it's really important to check what the latest information is on choices and routes and your options.

You should also realise that your parents, lecturers, tutors or mentors may have out-of-date information – check and check again with the employer or the professional organisation (for example, Royal Society, College, Association), career services, and the professional trade magazines. Even when you think you understand it, check it by trying to explain it to a friend, or run it by someone who ought to know, for example, a university careers adviser or the relevant trade association or college, or your potential employer.

Am I sure? How do I know that? These can be really powerful questions for you along the map route.

## DON'T PREDICT THE FUTURE

The third-year physics student was asking me to review a job application he wanted to send in later that week. As I started reading the job description, he said, 'I'm applying even though I know I won't get it, but it's good practice.'

Since I didn't really need practice in reviewing job applications, and I wasn't convinced that he would benefit from this application practice, and especially not from the apparently foretold rejection, I stopped reading and asked him, 'How do you know you won't get it?'

If he didn't really believe it, and it was a form of defence mechanism, then this behaviour didn't feel very productive, and was certainly not attractive. If, however, he really did believe it, then the obvious conclusion was not to waste time on the application. My real question to him, though, was, 'How do you know? Can you truly predict the future?'

Unless you have a crystal ball with perfect results, then make sure you are not predicting what will happen as a result of your action. Give-away phrases include: 'They won't want to meet', 'They'll never hire me', 'They'll hire someone else', 'They won't pay enough', and so on.

You may well be right, and sometimes it can be commendable to make a realistic assessment of your chances; however, with job applications and networking requests, you are dealing with other human beings and therefore with emotions. Decisions in this field are rarely wholly quantifiable, rarely all-or-nothing; you are entering the world of persuasion where sometimes, if you say it, you can make it so.

This is not always a meritocracy where rewards go unquestioningly to the best candidate on paper; it can be difficult to adjust to this world where, to coin a phrase, you sometimes have to blag it, to act confident and successful, even if you are feeling otherwise. We are all attracted to success, and repelled by failure – in terms of projects, people say that 'success has many parents and failure is an orphan'. So it is with working with people – we all want to work with people who make us feel good and are positive and energetic. This is not to say that we don't understand that things don't always work out, but we like people who recognise realistically if things haven't been perfect, are open about what happened, and are ready to see what to do to fix things.

**Success breeds success**

In 1968, sociologist Robert Morton observed that in science, those who were doing well would accumulate more funding and more success. He called this the Matthew effect, after the verse in the Bible (Matthew 13:12) 'For whosoever hath, to him shall be given, and he shall have more abundance: but whosoever hath not, from him shall be taken away even that he hath.'

More recently, Arnaut van de Rijt at Stony Brook University, New York State, ran an experiment by randomly distributing 'success' in the form of donations or positive ratings on four websites like Kickstarter and Change.org. They found that small initial random success led to eventual greater results than those control subjects that did not get the initial donations or ratings. One might say that the projects that received van de Rijt's largesse got lucky.

In the absence of an external donor, you have to make your own luck, like the busker who puts some of his own money in the hat to show potential supporters that others apparently already rated him.

WHERE AM I GOING AND CAN I HAVE A MAP?

Back to predicting the future: one very practical reason not even to voice the 'I'll never get, they won't pick me' view of the world is that it can become a self-fulfilling prophecy. If you say it, it will worm its way into your brain – saying things out loud somehow gives ideas more legitimacy – and you could well start sending explicit or subtle signals to give them enough reasons to reject you. If you find yourself predicting the future, stop, recognise what you are doing and consider all the possible futures and what you might do for each possibility.

## WHAT WENT WRONG?

You've been for an interview, sent in an application, met someone for a networking chat, spent time in an assessment centre, or phoned someone to ask for a meeting – and it didn't go well. You didn't get the job, the application was ignored, the networking gave you no new information or new contacts, you were asked to leave the assessment centre at the lunch break, or the person you called for a meeting has ignored you or refused to take your call.

What went wrong? Is it you, or them? It's probably going to be difficult to tell (unless you made a real humdinger of a mistake) though it will be worth thinking about. While you know what you did, and what they did, you don't usually know their decision-making process – why did they decide not to meet you, not to shortlist you, or not to give you a good Information Interview?

Assuming their default position is Do Nothing, then somehow you have failed to persuade them to Do Something. Of course, it may have been an explicit performance failure on your part, for example, you didn't score highly enough on the aptitude tests – in which case you will know what you did wrong, and can work on doing better at the tests next time.

**Perhaps the feedback is right**

The student had booked a one-to-one meeting for some interview practice. 'Thing is,' she said, 'I've not been getting past the online tests so not been called for interview yet.'

'Have you had any feedback from the tests?' I asked.

'Yes, apparently I'm very strong on relationship building and negotiation, but not scoring highly enough on maths and logic tests – but I can work really hard to get better at those.'

I decided to look at the feedback in the other way. 'What if you take the feedback as a valuable insight into your strengths? What if you play to your strengths and look at jobs that require good relationship building and negotiation? And not try to force fit yourself to this other role that clearly does not suit your strengths?'

It only took her a few seconds to think about this significant change in direction, and then she was visibly relieved.

Taking the case where you have failed to persuade them to do something for you (rather than nothing), the next question is whether there was something else you could have done to get a different outcome? Was it:

★ What you did? Usually this will be something you said, or perhaps didn't say.
★ How, when or where you did it? Though this seems unlikely to make someone change their mind about you unless it shows a lack of some social skill on your part; perhaps you misjudged a social situation and asked for a business contact, or asked them in front of other people so they couldn't say 'No'.
★ Who did it? If it's because of who you are, then can you change this? Obviously you can't change yourself, so I mean is it your reputation? Something they believe

about you that they don't like? How do they know? Is it on Facebook? Is it true? If not, can you try changing their opinion by explaining about your reputation?

Think about all the factors and clinically assess the likelihood that each had an effect. If it is something you did, then you could try to address what went wrong and ask again, or at the very least, note what happened and try not to repeat it. If it wasn't what you said or did, then ask what it might tell you about them.

First, are you ever going to get anywhere with them? The answer is important because if you think there's a low chance of changing their mind, then they represent the proverbial large hole in one particular road – you do not want to fall into it again, and the hole isn't going anywhere, so find a different road.

Second, would you want to work for someone like that? Probably not. Lucky escape!

There is another explanation: you did nothing wrong, asked the right questions, performed at the target level in the tests, but on the day, there genuinely was someone else who they thought was even better. If you didn't get the job, and you did as well as you could, then don't despair and throw away all your technique; if you do decide to do anything differently, you could try to find out more about what the interviewers are looking for so that next time, you can be the best candidate on the day.

## OVERCOMING PREJUDICE

*Prejudice: forming an opinion before becoming aware of the facts.*

This might be based on previous experience ('They're all like that'), by gossip and rumour-mongering ('I've heard that'), or by some learned behaviour. Whatever the cause, if you run into prejudice, you will be treated unfairly and, perhaps, illegally.

Around the world, there is some protection in law against prejudice. In the UK, there are nine so-called *Protected Characteristics* enshrined in the Equality Act 2010. Under the act, an employer or recruiter cannot legally discriminate against an applicant on the basis of their age*, disability, gender reassignment, marital status, pregnancy or maternity, race, religion or beliefs, sex, and sexual orientation. One or more of these will apply to you and it can be a real shock, if you have never been exposed to prejudice, suddenly to run into it – either because your circumstances have changed, or you're meeting new people in a new industry with different, er, customs.

So much for the legally protected characteristics, what about other, unspoken, prejudices? Here we enter a real minefield (did I mention there were minefields on the map?). I include physical characteristics like height or weight, regional accent, how you dress, and also intangible characteristics such as educational background, social class, previous success, and personal reputation. While we're on the subject, we could include beauty, personal wealth, partner's status, car and so on. We are into the murky world of Shakespeare's green-eyed monster here. No one is going to confess to this publicly or in writing (though there have been one or two notable exceptions, thanks to social media) but, unfortunately, they exist behind closed doors.

As we tiptoe into the minefield, what might the results be from the unspoken and hidden prejudices?

★ If you are a young woman, are they thinking 'Will she go off on maternity leave for a year?'
★ If you've driven up in an expensive or new car, are they thinking 'Does this person really need the job?'

*Age isn't quite totally free: it can be OK to treat someone differently because of their age.

★ If you have a physical disability, affecting your sight, hearing or mobility, are they thinking 'Will this person cope? What changes will we have to make? At what cost?'

★ If you come from a different background or social class or have a regional accent, are they thinking 'Will this person fit in? How will this person be with our clients?'

★ If they have heard rumours that you're 'difficult to work with,' are they thinking 'Is this person trouble?'

★ If they think you 'have it all' (such as education, good looks, confidence, and previous success), are they thinking 'This person doesn't deserve it'?

★ If they think you are highly intelligent with a great degree from a leading university, are they thinking 'This person might outshine me'?

### Queen Bee syndrome

First defined in 1973, the Queen Bee syndrome describes a woman in a position of authority who treats people who report to her more critically if they are female. In other words, she doesn't want other women around who might threaten her; it has been suggested that women who have progressed to a high position in a male-dominated organisation have done so by demonstrating 'masculine' traits – and feel they have to continue to do so with young female staff.

Choosing when, and what, to disclose can be a tricky decision. If you have a physical or hidden disability, when should you reveal this? You don't want to run the risk of being discriminated against (regardless of the legal position), but you also want to appear open and honest. For some disabilities, you may need potential employees to make some allowances at the interview, or assessment and, in the longer term, in the workplace. I think in this case you may leave it until you need to tell them. So wait until you are called for an interview, then tell them about, say, your mobility problems. Since it's likely that whatever it is you need to tell them is a protected characteristic, it's also likely that they have already made adjustments and be ready to accommodate you.

When it comes to the unspoken prejudices, a first step is to recognise they exist and then do what you can to avoid giving them the evidence. Is this being dishonest? No, since all the hidden prejudices are irrelevant to whether you can do the job. When you are trying to get the job, don't become over-principled: 'I'm going to show them exactly who I am'.

If you are concerned that they may think you've had 'all the luck', then you can disarm this with 'I've been extremely lucky to have...' No false modesty please:

'I play a little tennis.'

'Weren't you in junior Wimbledon last year?'

'Oh, yes, but it was nothing really.'

And, of course, there are plenty of stories of women taking off wedding rings before interviews – even though what they get up to outside work is none of the interview panel's business.

If asked tricky questions that imply someone is seeking background information to address their own biases, then ignore or deflect the question. In the last resort, you can say:

'I'd be very happy to discuss that outside this interview, if I'm offered the job.'

At another level, you could ask if the person is asking all the candidates that question.

What else can you do if faced with hidden prejudice? There is an inevitable, no-win conflict between you complaining – and being seen as 'difficult' – and putting up with it, and not getting appointed. If you have the choice, then you'll walk away – why would you work for such an organisation? If you get really attuned to this, you won't waste your own time even applying.

> **Pedigree: How Elite Students Get Elite Jobs**
>
> In Lauren Rivera's 2015 book, she reported on Wall Street firms' recruiting practices and showed that, far from being a pure meritocracy, considerable unspoken biases apply to select people with a similar cultural fit. Or, as Margaret Thatcher frequently asked, 'Are you one of us?'
>
> One finding was that men from upper-middle-class backgrounds with an interest in team sports did particularly well. Rather than wholly criticising the opaque and distorted approach, *The Economist* magazine took the view that this offered a good insight for applicants into how to secure such jobs.

At some point, you have a choice: adjust your own behaviour to fit in, with the idea that once you're in a position of power you will revert back to your true self and work to change the organisation; or decide that there's too much adjustment and you're better off elsewhere where you can show the first group that you can beat them.

## DON'T REPEAT ACTIONS, UNLESS YOU WANT THE SAME RESULT

Variously attributed to Albert Einstein and Mark Twain, it is somewhat of a truism to say that if you want the same outcome, keep taking the same action, or, as Einstein may or may not have said, 'Insanity is doing something over and over again and expecting a different result.'

If your CV and letter are not getting you the results you want, consider changing one or the other, or both. If emails alone are not getting you an Information Interview, try phoning. If you are called for interview, making it through various assessment centres, but not getting the job offer, then think about changing your interview technique. If any of these have happened a few times, in different organisations, and you are the only common factor in all these cases, then it may be time to consider the way you are acting as a likely cause of the issue.

To paraphrase Portia Nelson's famous short poem, beloved of self-help groups: if you keep walking down the same street and falling into the same hole in that street, you'd do well to choose a different street, rather than fighting the unmoving hole in the same street.

## Cats and dogs

There is a general belief that people's behaviour can be characterised as either like a cat or a dog, and there have been several academic research studies, involving large samples of people, which seem to support the theory. In any event, it is a neat model and, as far as your career and job seeking is concerned, can give you another tool to use.

If you think about it, dogs are very loyal, seem to want to obey their masters, enjoy being rewarded for doing well, and relish repetitive tasks. Throw the stick, they bring it back, again and again and again. Most people usually behave in this dog-like way, and employers like to recruit 'dogs'.

On the other hand, cats are their own masters: throw a ball, they ignore it; however, if you tease them with paper on a string, continually pulling it just out of reach, they love it – but if you let them get it, they get bored easily and wander off. In fact, one minute they're sitting on your lap asleep, the next, they've jumped down and walked off. Senior people are like cats – they respond to being intrigued, not just being given the whole story.

The lesson for you, when trying to get a senior person's attention is to treat them like a cat – intrigue them, give them some of the story, then sit back and don't appear too needy. Since most of us behave like dogs, especially when we're junior and trying to attract a senior person's attention, we think we have to do everything really well, to earn respect. The paradox for the 'dogs' is that by doing exactly what is asked, or even more than is asked, the 'cats' are grateful but because we don't intrigue them, we don't earn all their respect. So try to be more cat-like, and watch the results.

And in the spirit of this book, having finally come to terms with the fact that it may be that you have to change your actions and behaviours because you really want to get a different result, what to do? Some ideas:

★ Consider a training course, for example on interview technique where you can practise, be videoed and have your approach professionally critiqued.
★ Have someone else read your CV, cover letter, etc.
★ Talk to people about the situation – here you'll need an 'honest friend', not afraid to give you some difficult messages; your mentor might be good here, but better would be someone new and impartial; your school or university careers advisers would fit this bill, even if it's several years since you left.
★ Video yourself – easy now that laptops, tablets, and smartphones all have cameras. Critique yourself. Consider subscribing to online services that are populated with interview questions.
★ Discuss your career plan and strategies for making it happen with someone – friends can be good here as they

know you, your strengths and weaknesses; a career coach will need time to get to know you, but may then challenge you more widely.

★ Be brave! Try something new the next time; see what happens. Information Interviews are the ideal time as they are low risk, because a job is not (usually or directly) riding on the result.

## WHERE ARE THE BOUNDARIES?

I had been talking to a student about their forthcoming interview and how to approach case studies. We'd been through an example, and I'd commented on what she had done well, and areas that she might want to think about.

'Overall,' I asked her, 'what is your task at this interview?'

'To get a job offer,' she said, 'that's why I'm doing this.'

'Is that in your control, do you think?'

'Well, not completely.'

Assuming you've grown up with other people around you, probably sharing the same building, you'll be used to the idea of boundaries – what you're responsible for and what others are responsible for. It's a useful concept in the area of jobs, identifying the boundaries between the things that you are responsible for, and those functions for which others are responsible.

### Zone of Control

You can think of this as three concentric circles: the innermost circle is the area, or zone, of the world that you fully control; the ring outside your zone of control, contains things and activities that you can influence even if not fully control; and the outer ring contains things over which you have no control. Clearly the outer ring is by far the biggest since it contains everything in the world; by contrast the innermost circle will have only those aspects that you control directly – such as what you eat, what you wear, what music you listen to, and so on.

It can be a great relief to realise that some things are not in your zone of control, even if you are very concerned about them: I might include world famine, malaria, national economic performance, and nuclear weapon proliferation in this. The influence zone might contain your friends and family.

When we think about the interview that the student was facing, inside her zone of control was her performance at the interview, outside her control was whether she was offered the job. To put it another way, when you go for an interview or a meeting, your responsibility is to represent yourself in the most accurate and best light to the interviewer(s); their responsibility is to decide whether to hire you. Since the hiring decision is not your responsibility, don't try to take it on.

This idea can help at work and outside work in your social life, understanding and recognising what you can and cannot control. For example, you can try to arrange meetings with someone, email and phone, offer several choices of date, but in the end they have to decide whether to meet. If they choose not to meet you, well, it's disappointing but not in your control so you may decide to move on, or come at it another way (see the section on 'No' doesn't mean never).

The reverse also applies: if someone offers you a job or a meeting, or invites you to do some work for them, then you decide whether to do it or not; it is your responsibility to make that decision. The alternative is that you sign up for something that you don't really want to do; unless there are good reasons such as getting to know the organisation or impressing someone important to you, then you'll probably not perform at your best and be wishing you were somewhere else.

## DON'T LOOK BACK . . . EXCEPT TO REFLECT

After events, it is human nature to look back and try to draw lessons from what happened. Especially when bad things happened, like not being offered a job after an interview, not being shortlisted, missing an application deadline, not being promoted and so on: all events where some desired outcome did not happen. It can be, in the shock and disappointment, all too easy to draw conclusions such as 'I'm no good at interviewing', or 'I never get jobs', or 'I always miss the deadlines'.

> **Never?**
>
> 'Always, never, every time' are strong descriptions that are easily used and send a crushing and dispiriting message that the results of your actions are pre-ordained – yet these descriptions are rarely true.
>
> If you find yourself using phrases like, 'This always happens', then stop yourself and check: Always? 100 per cent? Every single time? Ah, thought not.

It's easy to write here, but not always so easy to remember at the time, that looking back and drawing conclusions like these will undermine your confidence and probably not be at all accurate. Try not to look for patterns that are just coincidence or have a temporal rather than a causal connection. It's most likely that there will be too many different external factors for you to discern a pattern, unless you are being overly selective about the data you include – beware the Texas sharpshooter.

## The Texas sharpshooter fallacy

An informal fallacy that occurs when similarities in data are stressed (for example, outcomes of interviews) and differences in the data are ignored (for example, different organisations, different types of candidate sought, and so on).

The name comes from the idea of a Texan who fires a number of shots at a barn door, then runs round the other side of the door and draws a target round the densest cluster of holes to show he is a really accurate shot.

What to do? If possible, let your emotion die down after you receive an unwanted result. Talk it through with other people, ideally who are not (too) emotionally connected. Reflect realistically on what happened – think hard about whether you could have performed any better, done anything that was within your control any better. If so, that could be a very useful lesson for next time. It might also point you towards some skills you could work on before the next interview. Perhaps you hadn't done enough background research on the organisation, or answered interview questions clearly and succinctly enough. So next time, you'll know to do more research, perhaps in a different way, and in the meantime, seek out some interview practice – maybe even go on a course.

When you are reflecting on why you weren't shortlisted or didn't pass the interview, yet cannot genuinely think of something that you messed up seriously, consider the simplest solution. This might confirm that, despite your very good performance, through no fault of your own, they were looking for someone with a different skill-set or style that they couldn't work out, or perhaps even know, without meeting you in interview.

As always, it can be helpful to ask for feedback; while they may not be able or wish to tell you that they changed their mind, or they just preferred someone else, you could ask some detailed questions about elements of your interview or application – and always not because you are challenging their decision (you should make that clear) but because you'd value their honest opinion so you can improve for next time.

'But I did everything right. Great CV and cover letter, good application form, I got called for interview, and that seemed to go OK, I got on really well with the interviewers, the assessment centre seemed to be fine, but I've just got this rejection!' said the final-year student to me during a one-to-one session last year. 'What did I do wrong?' he asked.

We looked over his application and the job description, though since he'd been called for interview, clearly the application, CV, and assessment centre were enough to get him selected for the next stage. In the end, we concluded that he probably did nothing wrong; perhaps the employer changed their mind, perhaps they had ten excellent applicants for three places, perhaps they had a specific type of candidate in mind but were not able (or willing) to declare that. Obviously this latter reason is unfair and difficult to counter – but you can learn from such an experience by asking about the type of candidate they are looking for in the interview or, ideally, before the application.

Finally, when things go well, you get called for interview, you get the job, or you make a great connection, spend time reflecting on that: what did you do that made it work out? Was it luck again, or was there something you did or said, some action you took, that generated the positive outcome? If so, be sure to remember to do that again at the right time and situation.

## OTHER PEOPLE

We humans can be competitive creatures, whether inherent in our nature or trained through education and sport; we can measure our performance against our own previous performance, against an absolute standard or against other people. The last comparison can be flawed, but feel very powerful.

Who amongst us hasn't looked across and thought something like, 'My classmates have landed great jobs, are paid really well, work pretty good hours, and are having a great social life'?

Who are these perfect people? How would we know all this? Are we sure they aren't working all hours, have large and growing overdrafts, and no time for a social life? An exaggeration and caricature perhaps, but even if that were all true, so what? Would you swap places, if you could?

We have asymmetric information – we know everything (well, a lot) about ourselves, and very little about other people, and we have to recognise that we only know what they have chosen to let us know about them. We also are subject to what sociologists call *confirmation bias*; the tendency to search for and recall information that supports our beliefs, while giving much less consideration to alternative possibilities. It's why the other queues at the supermarket checkout always seem to move faster than the one we are in.

### The friendship paradox

First observed by sociologist Scott L. Field in 1991, this is the phenomenon that most people have fewer friends than their friends have. Before you get too depressed, you can take consolation in the fact that there is a perfectly good mathematical explanation (good, but not simple – I commend you to the relevant Wikipedia pages if you want to know more). I also find helpful and compelling the explanation from psychologist Satoshi Kanazawa that people with more friends are just more likely to be friends with you, or (turning it round) that you're more likely to know more popular people.

The generalised 'friendship paradox' takes this idea and expands it to explain why people at the gym are fitter than you (the less fit ones don't go to the gym), people in your book club are better read, and the co-authors on your papers have more publications than you.

So bear this in mind when you compare yourself, your progress, your success and failures with others. Warning signs are phrases along the lines of 'Everyone else is doing better than me', or 'This doesn't happen to anyone else'. There's another discussion here about the use of absolutes like 'everyone' or 'no one'; such phrases can be used in the heat of the moment ('everyone else seems to have a job') but, annoying as it may be, it can be helpful to check if it really is everyone . . . in the whole world? . . . or even amongst your class? . . . your friends? . . . your neighbours?

Comparisons with absolute measures, and with ourselves over time, all have their place: they spur us on and challenge our thinking. But comparisons with others are based on superficial, perhaps inaccurate, and incomplete information. Friends with whom we are comparing ourselves also have feet of clay and, perhaps luckily, we never know what goes on behind closed doors.

Discussions of comparisons can be helpful in showing you particularly what you'd like to change in your own life. 'Some of my friends seem to be in jobs that make them happy; they come alive when they talk about them and seem really quite fulfilled. I don't feel like that about my job; I want to feel like they do, I wonder what it is they're doing, how they got there and what compromises they have made?'

## MENTORS AND SPONSORS
## – HELP IS AT HAND

The idea of having a mentor to help you in your career is, in some ways, not new; the original 'mentor' is described in Homer's

*Odyssey,* in which the goddess Athena takes on the role of mentor to guide Telemachus on his journey. We aren't always so lucky as to have a goddess as our mentor, and from what I remember, when mortals engage with the Greek gods, it doesn't usually end well for the mortals.

Back in the real world, a mentor can play a role of helping you in your career quest; they usually have more experience in an industry or in a specific organisation, and understand general processes or projects you are working on. In a nutshell, they've seen it before. They are usually about the same age or older and bring a wisdom that can help you overcome an obstacle, unblock your thinking, suggest an alternative direction, consider some options, or provide specific ideas for how to handle a particular situation. They will be an honest friend and should not be afraid to discuss something you may initially find unwelcome. You may have more than one mentor, and you may use them sporadically (spurred on by a certain problem you are facing) or regularly, if infrequently.

An initial stage of mentoring can be passive: observing people you work with, know or see on TV or in films, and thinking, 'I'd like to behave like, act like, or be like that.' You don't have to want to be like the whole person, but you could pick and choose particular aspects of people's characters that you admire and would wish to emulate. It might be a:

★ Hostage negotiator demonstrating an effective way of handling a crisis
★ Scientist persisting at experiments that are not yet working
★ Football manager developing the whole team
★ Business leader explaining the strategy for their industry
★ Colleague in a meeting who seems to be able to get their point across without upsetting people, or (better) bringing people along with them

Unlike Athena, your real-life mentor will not suddenly appear by your side, in your moment of need. You'll need to find one for yourself; having a mentor assigned to you does not usually work nearly as well as if you find someone who suits you and is definitely interested in supporting you. How to find a mentor?

As you go through your working day, you may decide that one or two of the people you work with and who seem to have more experience in your field could offer you considerable and valuable help on a one-to-one basis. They may be in your current organisation, in a rival organisation, working as an independent consultant to your industry, or a speaker you were impressed with at a conference.

You could either develop a relationship informally, asking to meet them for advice and so forth, or you could ask them if they would consider being a mentor – or the first step could lead to the second, of course. It's worth being open about what you do expect from a mentor:

★ Honest advice and insight
★ Suggestions on how to unblock or avoid obstacles
★ Act as a sounding board for your ideas and plans
★ Be available from time to time, not immediately and not too frequently

Just as important is that you do *not* expect your mentor to:

★ Find you a job
★ Word edit your CV, cover letter and other application material
★ Provide a reference
★ Introduce you to contacts
★ Drop everything when you call

While the idea of a mentor has been around in business for about twenty years, more recently some have been saying that what you might really need is a sponsor – the difference being that a sponsor will open (metaphorical) doors and promote your case to others who might be in a position to advance your career.

Even when your career is running along smoothly, perhaps you've just got that new job or promotion, you can still greatly benefit from having a mentor – and they will enjoy and feel rewarded from mentoring someone as open and receptive as you.

## THE OTHER SIDE (TIME RUNS AT DIFFERENT SPEEDS)

Before the days of mobile phones, and before the days of voice-mail or answerphones, it was not unheard of for people to stay in, 'sitting by the phone' waiting for it to ring. Now we can be reached anywhere and although the usual lament in magazine articles is how 'one can never disconnect', mobile phones have given us enormous flexibility. The work–home boundary has, if one wishes, become more porous; we no longer have to stay in and wait by any phone, the phone comes with us – whether at work or not.

We are used to not waiting: time was you had to wait whole days for the post to arrive with that precious job offer, now we expect to get the phone call within hours of the interview (and indeed I have heard of people getting an offer while they were on the bus on their way home from the meeting). While the time between the decision being made and you receiving an offer has got shorter (it's the time to receive an email or phone call now, compared with a couple of days for them to type, check, then post a letter), the decision process probably hasn't got any shorter. And it's the decision process that takes up most of the time.

For example, the interview team might all have dispersed after your interview or assessment centre to catch up on the work they missed, then there was a public holiday, one member went on a couple of days' annual leave, the senior executive who signs off the formal offer was in meetings in London for two days, the annual budget round needed to be completed, and an urgent request from the CEO just arrived. All of these contributed to a week or more going by without them noticing. Your job decision and offer will get to the top of the pile but only once more urgent matters that keep the business running have been completed.

In other words, when you're waiting to hear about a job or Information Interview, time seems to crawl by. 'It's been three days!', but remember that time is going faster for them with many other activities to complete, while you're really focused on this decision.

One way to cope with this is to distract yourself. Sitting around waiting won't usually make it happen any quicker so you could finish an essay, write some letters to friends, visit an art gallery, play some sport, or buy the ingredients and cook a meal from a new recipe.

However, if it's been two weeks and you still haven't heard then you should feel able to check in on the status of your request or job application, in a neutral way.

'I came for interview two weeks ago, and I wondered when I could expect to hear the outcome?'

'I wrote last week asking if X would consider sparing fifteen minutes for an Information Interview, and wondered if we could confirm a date for that?'

What's the worst that could happen? Possible responses to your question include:

'Sorry, we've all been really busy, we are aiming to let you know by the end of the week.'

'I don't think we ever received that email asking for an Information Interview; could you send it again or let me know what it's about and we could sort something out now?'

'We wrote to you last week, didn't you get the letter? I'll send it again.'

'We lost your paperwork and contact details, so I'm glad you called.'

'We're not going to take your application any further and it's our policy not to let people know unless we do take things further.'

This last one does give you the chance to answer 'OK, thanks for letting me know that; it would be really helpful for me if I could have some feedback so I can improve my chances in future – would you, or a colleague, be able to give me that?'

A very unlikely response to your enquiry is:

'Oh, well, we were about to offer you the job, but as you've just called up we're not going to do that now. Goodbye.'

I think that what might stop people chasing up applications or requests is the fear of getting this last, rather quixotic, answer, but it does look very, very unlikely, doesn't it? And if someone did tell you that, would you want to work for them?

## HOW DO YOU FEEL?

'You know that time at the end of an interview, when they say, "Do you have any questions for us?", well, what do you think I should ask?' is a common question from students when we're discussing a forthcoming interview.

'All these companies look the same,' said the student at the doors of the Careers Fair, 'what should I talk to them about? What do I want to know?'

When you meet someone, face to face, who works somewhere you might be employed at for several years, it gives you the chance to ask things that are difficult, if not impossible, to write down in brochures and on websites. It is invaluable to learn about the *culture* of the organisation. You might ask questions like:

★ 'Can you describe the organisation in one word?'
★ 'Why do you work here?'
★ 'What does it feel like working here?'
★ 'What three things get you out of bed in the morning to keep you coming into work at this organisation?'
★ 'If you have ideas or specific suggestions on how to improve things or do something new, would there be a chance for you to try them out?'

When you have listed all the practical reasons for and against the organisation and the new role, and compared it with other choices or your current situation, you will still be faced with an unquantifiable element – how it feels to work there. Your list will not be perfect either, and it will contain uncertainties around how the organisation will change in the future, but it will have helped you identify why you are attracted to the new position.

Even if you can't articulate it immediately, if the organisation or its people don't feel right to you, then trust your feelings, if only to force yourself to explore why you are feeling that way.

Go back to the section on 'What do you want?', and see if the people and organisation you met feel like they will support your ambitions. Are they supportive? Forgiving? Encouraging?

WHERE AM I GOING AND CAN I HAVE A MAP?

Open? Ready to give you responsibility? To train you? Or, on the other hand, do you suspect they are controlling? Measuring your performance closely? Going to keep you in your place? Unsupportive?

These are necessarily black and white opposites – I exaggerate for effect – but the first sort of behaviours are more likely to keep you interested in the work, give you a sense of purpose and reward.

On the flip side, if you are really excited about the organisation and people, then force yourself to explain all this to a colleague or friend who will challenge you and maybe play Devil's advocate. Keep an open mind when they share their thoughts; you may still follow your heart, but at least you'll be aware and maybe use their ideas to negotiate.

In the end, you will have an imperfect set of incomplete information – some of it quantifiable (for example, pay, commuting time, hours, reporting lines) and most of it descriptive and based on feelings. At some point, you will have to trust your feelings, especially if you hear people say, 'It feels like a great place to work.' There's no answer in the back of the book and you are the only person who can make the decision (helped perhaps by talking it over with others), but give yourself credit, take the responsibility and trust your decision.

## DON'T GIVE UP

Of course, you're not going to give up – you can't give up for one thing, because you really do want to get a job, or more likely because you really do need a job; if you're already in a job, looking for the next step on your career path across the map, then you might take your foot off the gas and be tempted to settle for not moving, but then you realise, 'No, I really *do* want to change my job.'

It can be a long, hard road across the career map. One issue is that it can feel 'all or nothing'; you've either got a job or you haven't – there's no middle ground and you can't be a bit unemployed. You can, of course, be underemployed – and if this is your long-term situation, then it's time to get going. When you haven't got a job, and no interviews on the horizon, or new roles to apply for, it can start to feel extremely dark.

You may have been working really hard, sending many applications, arranging networking meetings, finding a mentor, and getting interviews and still it's not paying off. It just may not be possible to predict the success factors – it is very difficult for all of us to predict what is essentially a serendipitous process. And while the old joke of one Jewish mother to another about her son, 'You know, the harder he works, the luckier he gets,' has some truth, there is also an element of luck. Call it the alignment of the stars, or 'right place, right time', it's out of your control. So, in an interpretation of the phrase that hard work generates luck, make sure you have lots of irons in the fire, as you'll increase your chances of luck striking.

### Reward yourself

Even if things aren't working out the way you wanted, be kind to yourself and give yourself some rewards for effort. The day of the interview, plan to go to the movies in the evening; after you've made all your calls for the day or filled in another application, go to the gym or for a run or to a museum.

As the financial service providers say in their ads, the past is no indicator of future performance. That new person you are meeting today is a blank sheet for you to write your story on; they don't know about the blind alleys you've followed or rejections you've had. Many times you'll have to be like an actor in a long-running play – every audience is new, and expecting a great performance.

It will be a different performance each time as you'll be polishing your words and techniques, learning what worked and what didn't, and applying new ideas and knowledge.

## MAKE TIME FOR NON-JOB ACTIVITIES

Finding a job can feel like a job in itself, and if you are unemployed, it can become an all-consuming job in itself. Your day may settle into some sort of routine: check emails and write responses; research companies, people and jobs; search job websites; rewrite your CV; and phone possible contacts. Now and again, you will travel to meet people for Information Interviews, or to attend job interviews or assessment centres, then return to the constant round of emails and website searches.

Despite the ability to be checking emails and the Internet twenty-four hours a day, at some point each day you'll have done everything you can to move all your job-related actions forward. Now it is important to take a break, turn off the phone and computer, and give your mind a rest. Of course, that might be just the moment that someone chooses to call you with the most amazing job offer; so? You're a busy person, they'll leave a message and, since they are busy as well, they won't expect you to be able to respond instantly. You're busy and successful. A couple of hours' time, or even tomorrow, will be OK – in fact, it might even be better than responding within seconds. So, it's all right to be away from your desk and phone. Now, what to do?

**Things to do**

★ Visit a new museum/art gallery/shop/city/sports ground/club

★ Burn off your adrenaline with sport – one you already do or take up a new one

★ Develop your mind by learning a new language or a new skill with a musical instrument

★ Learn to make bread, or to build brick walls

★ Volunteer at the local hospital or primary school

★ Teach someone one of your skills – be it reading or how to work a computer

★ Timetable these activities and commit them to your diary: 'I can't make that time as I'm volunteering at the local school.'

Meeting up with friends might be problematic. If they are working, and you are not, it may not do much for your self-esteem (and on a practical level they may not be free when you are); if they are also job-hunting, then it might help you to act as mentor or adviser to them, reviewing their CV or challenging their search strategies and so on.

When you are out of work and searching for a job, it can feel lonely and perhaps desperate. A job is one of those things that is all or nothing, you can't half have a job (though you can have half a job, of course). Getting out and about, exploring new places and meeting new people can demonstrate that you are not defined just as a job seeker, and can be encouraging as you make progress in some activities – this progress can boost your confidence and, who knows, that might spill over into the job search.

Finally, when you do get a job, you'll look back and wish that you'd spent even 5 per cent of that period doing other things that, now you're in work, you just don't have the time for any more. How much better to be able to say, 'You know, during that three months of looking for work, I managed to visit four major art galleries / play football most Wednesday afternoons / help five children in the local school to read.'

## IT CAN BE DARK AND DESPAIRING IF ACTIONS HAVE NOT YIELDED RESULTS

When you set out to design and then cross your career map, you'll know that it may not be straightforward – that there may be dark and difficult times. At the start, it's tough to believe and really feel that your job search might get quite daunting and depressing and I hope it won't, but just in case it does, if you remember that you did think it *might* happen, hopefully, it won't be too much of a shock.

The job search, or career change, is not all relentlessly positive and fulfilling; getting knocked back, several times, can be depressing. It's not true that if you just Think Positive, great things will happen. Bumper stickers are just that, a few words that make you smile – human behaviour is more complicated than being summed up in a few words.

Some ideas on how to divert yourself and look at your career map again:

★ Go back over all your notes – you may spot a contact you never followed up, or who it might be worth checking in with.
★ Do some activity (play the drums, game of football, wash the car, mow the lawn) that is also giving yourself permission to take a break and come back refreshed, perhaps with new ideas from the unconscious mind that have been given the space to bubble through.
★ Put yourself somewhere new – be it sport, museum, club, social activity, or a part of town where you don't normally go.
★ Go to a library or bookstore and give yourself permission

to browse for an hour in a section that you don't usually go to. Re-read a book off your shelves.

★ Review your plan with a friend – a problem shared is not a problem solved but instead is one where you get twice the number of possible solutions.

It's understandable that you will feel anxious about the lack of job success, and that anxiety may be increasing because of outside pressures. The best way, psychologists will tell you, to reduce anxiety about a specific concern, is to start working on that concern. Whether it is a job search, course assignment, essay, overdraft or parking ticket, putting your head in the sand only increases anxiety.

Given that, if you are looking to refresh your career map with a diverting activity, try to make it career or job related, rather than, say, a trip to the movies. That way it is diverting but you are also making some inroads on addressing the job in hand.

Finally, if you're not making progress, set yourself a deadline: you could, for example, give yourself three months to have made headway on your new direction and, if you haven't made sufficient progress by that date, you can stop. This way, you'll stay in control of your own career map. This isn't to say that you may not come back to this in a few months' time, but for now, you're going to try Plan B, a different route across the map.

# Afterword

It is natural that when you are in a job, or productively engaged in study as a student, this book and the actions described will go to the metaphorical and actual back of the top shelf to gather dust. Then, when a crisis strikes, either through an internal yearning for a better job or an external change of circumstances, the contents become really important again. But perhaps the time to read it is also when you are happily in a job, just to keep those networking skills alive; as surely as night follows day, you will want to or have to get back on the job-hunting and career consideration track at some point, and you'd have a flying start if your Information Interviewing skills were good and your contact book wasn't completely empty.

Job-hunting and career searching can be exhilarating and despairing – I hope that you will have found some useful and helpful ideas and overall general encouragement in these pages, and wish (to paraphrase the Irish saying) that your job-hunting-road rises up to meet you.

# Acknowledgements

Over the years, I realise that I have gathered from friends, family, and colleagues so many great ideas that have ended up in this book. I thank them for their pearls of wisdom, some of which we might have talked about twenty years ago, but are still fresh today. So thank you to:

Peter Ginnings for mentorship and close friendship over many, many years; Adrian Bullock for authorial support, encouragement and friendship; Tim Hailstone for entrepreneurial wisdom; Professor Sir Mike Gregory for trailblazing and an unerring ability to cut to the essence of the issue; Andy Gill and all the other P.E.T. students from Cambridge for insightful observations of working life; John Helding of Booz Allen San Francisco who first taught me about CVs and Information Interviews; David Palfreyman at New College for his unique and personal insight into Higher Education over many years; all my colleagues at the Oxford University Careers Service, at New College, and across Oxford University for careers discussions over the last few years; all the students I've worked with, supported and taught over the last few years; and to my friend and agent, Barbara Levy, who encouraged me to get these ideas down on paper.

Finally thank you to my wonderful and supportive children, Alexander and Imogen, and to my closest friend, muse, inspiration, and love of my life, Nicky.

# Further Reading

Some books and articles that I have enjoyed:

Eric Berne, *What Do You Say After You Say Hello*, London, 1975

Oliver Burkeman, *HELP!: How to Become Slightly Happier and Get a Bit More Done*, Edinburgh, 2011

Eliyahu M. Goldratt and Jeff Cox, *The Goal: A Process of Ongoing Improvement*, Farnham, 3rd edition, 2004

Patsy Rodenburg, *Presence: How to Use Positive Energy in Every Situation*, London, 2009

Barry Schwartz, Darrin R. Lehman, Sonya Lyubomirsky, John Monterosso, Andrew Ward and Katherine White, 'Maximizing versus Satisficing: Happiness Is a Matter of Choice', *Journal of Personality and Social Psychology*, vol. 83 (2002), no. 5, pp. 1178–97

# Index

Note: page numbers in **bold** refer to illustrations, page numbers in *italics* refer to information contained in tables.

what to take in 82
and your interests 52–3
your responsibilities in 83
*see also* Information
Interviewing
investment banking 22–3
invisible forces 25–8
Iyengar, Sheena 8

job advertisements 34–6
   newspaper 34
   online 34–5
job descriptions 86
job interviews *see* interviews
job motivations 4, 6, 43–4
job offers
   choice of 107–8
   details 105
   negotiating 104–5
   time to receiving 139–41
job rejections 121–3, 147–8
job selection criteria 35, 59, 65–6
jobs
   how to find 33–42
      cold calling 34, 36–7
      creating your own job 34,
         39–40
      executive searches 34, 38–9
      internal promotion 34, 41–2
      job advertisements 34–6
      networking 34, 37–8
   undesirable parts 48
Jung, Carl 16

Kanazawa, Satoshi 135

Kennedy, John F. 30
Keynote slides 99–100
knowledge, checking your 117–19

Laozi 12
lawyers 14–15
leadership skills *46*
leisure, making time for 145–7
Lepper, Mark 8
letter writing 68
   *see also* cover letters
life expectancy 24
life sentences, seeing decisions as
     12–15, 28–9
LinkedIn 38, 75
listening, active 72, 78
location, choice of 28
luck, making your own 37, 144
Lucky Dip method xiii

management consultancy 5
Map method xiii–xiv
   aerial view 1–31
   along the way 109–48
   exploring the map 49–50
   the map emerges from the fog
     47–50
   practicalities 33–108
   what's on the map 48–9
marriage 20–1
Maslow, Abraham 18
maths jobs 48–9
Matthew effect 120
maximisers 9–10, 34
mentors 109, 129, 136–9